The Edge of Her Feathers

a memoir

Kristen Alexandra Davis

SHE WRITES PRESS

Published 2024
Printed in the United States of America
Print ISBN: 978-1-64742-690-3
E-ISBN: 978-1-64742-691-0
Library of Congress Control Number: 2024906798

For information, address:
She Writes Press
1569 Solano Ave #546
Berkeley, CA 94707

Interior Design by Tabitha Lahr

She Writes Press is a division of SparkPoint Studio, LLC.

For Natalie

The author, age 9

"In ancient Greece, the three Fates, or Moerae, determined the destiny of each newborn child. Ancient mythologists elevated them to the position of half-goddesses, representing them as three distinct individuals: Clotho, Lachesis, and Atropos. One spun the thread of life, one wound it, and one cut it short.

As the personifications of change, the Moerae appear at the three most important moments in a man's life: at his birth, his marriage, and his death.

Their first appearance is on the third night after a baby's birth, when they come to foretell his future, give advice, and favour him with his birthmarks. Great care should be taken to prepare the house for their arrival. It should be well swept and a table should be neatly laid out with honey, bread, and three white almonds. (In certain areas of Greece, water, coins, and precious gifts are also placed beside the food.) The door should be left open, a light kept burning, and the house should be very quiet.

Once the Moerae have pronounced the child's fate, it cannot be changed."

—From *A Field Guide to the Little People*

The Hardest Part

March 1986

I t would be simplest just to say that I'd forgotten what had happened to me before, and that his death made me remember. But I'm not even sure if that's what happened, though it seemed that way at the time. A shock of recognition, disbelief. How could one forget something like that? You stop thinking about it and your life changes: all the new places, new bonds rush up to meet you. All the time you are becoming different from the person you were without even realizing it. The weeks and months add themselves silently to your memories. Then one day it comes back to you, in a sudden, shocked way, a picture as perfect and complete in your mind's eye as a photograph. That was how it was for me to remember what happened, like waking up from a dream.

It was one of the most beautiful days I had ever seen—that morning in March. It had brought a brilliant blue sky with masses of white clouds and the wind blowing in huge broken gusts. Sailboats covered the bay like tiny white moths on a canopy of blue leaves. Late in the morning, while I sat in a salon having golden streaks burned into my brown hair, he would have been standing on the bridge looking down into the water, or maybe out beyond to the place where the tides meet. He would have been surrounded by the Headlands, the ocean, the wind, and all the people, some in cars rushing past, in boats below, and walking along, oblivious to him. He may have been the only one on the West Walk at the time, because of the strength of the wind. While I waited for the strands of my hair to turn blonde, he would have been pausing to wonder, for an instant. I used to believe he took that moment to consider what it was going to be like.

Now, so many years later, I realize he might never have thought about the next few moments. He may have been thinking only of the past. Such questions plagued me in the weeks that followed. But I knew no one who could answer them.

To get to the West Walk from the point where his car was parked, you must take a staircase underneath the bridge and come up again on the other side by the ocean. I went down there once. After the car was found and we waited for him to come back, for his body to come back, I went there and listened to the sound of the water and the wind, and later, in the stairwell beneath the span, the sounds of the cars passing overhead, their deafening vibration on the steel and concrete.

You're not really meant to stop down there, underneath. It's a place just to go through and leave by itself, untouched, on the way to someplace else. But something down there held me and made me afraid to go on. That's how I ended up standing frozen, listening, while each moment seemed to stretch out endlessly: the noise and momentum, the rush and press of people, cars, and machinery perceived from a solitary, silent point that was my own body, motionless and concealed. In that corridor there is no hint of the world outside, except for the sounds that envelop one in an

THE EDGE OF HER FEATHERS

isolation too sudden and complete. I don't remember anything after that, or whether I ever made my way to the span on the ocean side. I have never been on the bridge before or since. For a time, they closed the corridor and there was no longer any access to the West Walk.

I wanted him to be alive, somewhere in the hills, to believe that he had fallen or was hurt, but at least not in the water, to believe that he was somewhere waiting to be found. We did not know about the letter until later. We held on to the possibility of his being alive, and you must wonder why—it was selfish, really. It was for the same reason that you don't like the sun to sink too fast beneath the horizon: you know that soon it will be night, the sky will be dark and close around you, all the beautiful colors will be gone, and you had wanted to stay there awhile longer. I felt for him the way one does about something beautiful that you want to last.

But he had not fallen by accident, and he was not waiting for us in the hills, and his body never came back with the tide. Someone had seen him jump. A week later his family held a memorial service. I drove alone from the house where Kelley and I lived, across the bay by another bridge, to a chapel in the hills on the northern side. There had been rain again, in the days between, but that day came cold and clear and beautiful, just like the one a week before.

That night, after the service, I would have the worst of the dreams, and afterward I would wonder where it had come from, thinking back about the daylight. I did not understand at first. I could not have said what was the hardest part of that afternoon, while the sun still caught the beads of rain that lay on the edges of leaves and in puddles on the ground.

From the chapel the bridge was visible in the distance at the mouth of the bay. But that was not the hardest part. The hardest part was not the way she shone so strangely, like a jewel, beneath her mantle of dense, airless fog. Not in seeing her through the window of the chapel, holding herself weightlessly above the waves with her perfect, majestic indifference. It was not the perfect blue of the sky or the whiteness of the clouds or the smell of wet earth outside the chapel or the wind and the aftermath of rain. It was something someone said.

We had gone outside and were standing on a lawn, and I looked up and saw Kelley standing across from me. She had just glanced up at the sky. Her dress was dark against the colors of the grass and the brilliant blue above her, a small black figure in a huge landscape. I saw her eyes and looked away quickly; their expression was like a wound in my own body. But I could not remember when the wound had gotten there or how it had opened again.

Sean

Later that night I was sitting in front of a fire, and you were there, waiting for word of how the funeral had been. In the year that we first met, you had traveled the world over, sailing alone for months at a time. I looked up to you, to your knowledge of aloneness and the sea. For the first time since we had known each other, I had no desire to trade places with you. I told you what had happened at the service, what I could remember. The things that seemed safe to say. Before I left, I asked you if they would ever find his body.

You looked at me with an expression that was a mixture of pain and surprise, as if the possibility of such a lapse of reasoning on my part was more than you could have imagined. After a moment you said, "Darien, his body is a piece of human flesh floating in the ocean . . . it's been there for a week . . . fish and shark feed on flesh floating in the ocean."

I was sitting on the edge of the couch, and you were in front of me, the fire burning behind you. Weeks before I had sat in the same place, and Aiden had been sitting across from me.

I'd thought of the water before and its natural effects. I had thought of Natalie Wood, floating off the coast of Malibu, facedown. I had never thought of what you were saying.

I said, "Isn't there any way he could have washed into a cove or somewhere else . . . and hasn't been found yet? Somewhere people don't go?"

I felt my heart sinking without knowing why it mattered, anyway. You explained, just as I knew you could, the tides. That was the last time I wondered about Aiden being found. I wouldn't need to keep waiting for some word.

I put what you had said out of my mind; your words were unbearable to me. Later that night, just before falling asleep, I was reaching for the light switch by the doorway when it struck me suddenly. I saw his eyes. I hadn't considered his eyes.

What comes to me too suddenly, what comes on too hard and fast, I let go of—the thoughts floating away to another place, gently, while I turn away, unable to bear them. After a while they begin to sink, covered over with depths of memory. I watch my own detachment with surprise. While I sleep and work, and play and laugh, something else is happening. Then, when I least expect it, the thoughts come back. I've wondered about this for a long time; it has happened before, and it happened again that night before I fell asleep. I thought of his eyes, once full of kindness, as I turned out the light. Later, while I slept, some part of me that had continued its quiet ruminations worked a strange alchemy. I floated underwater in a sea whose depths I had never seen before. And I had the dream about the crow.

The Crow / Der Haifischtraum

I dreamt I was at home again.

I dreamt that I was in my old room, and my sister, Mara, was with me. We were sitting on my bed together, the lace of the canopy suspended above our heads, our hands and knees almost touching. The golden light was there, and filled the room, filled the air above us.

I remember it this way. She said, "I think you should talk to someone," and watched me.

"I'm talking to you."

"No, I mean . . . because it was so sudden. It might begin to get hard for you."

"It's hard for everyone. Already," I told her.

I could see the two of us from my dreaming place, the lace of the canopy and the bedspread underneath us, myself in the room, looking at the lace in that light.

"I don't want to talk," I told her. "I don't want to be alone anymore."

And then, as though it were something I finally believed, I told her: "We're not meant to be alone for years and never touch someone. I want to see Michael again. I want to find Michael."

I wanted to go. So I left her, thinking that I would find him, but everything changed. I walked down the hallway, but it was not a single house anymore. My steps led past rooms from different houses I had lived in, all of them suddenly appearing again in one place. At the end was a bedroom, the door ajar, and Michael was inside. I went to stand at the door of the room we had shared together in his house the year before, when I was twenty-two, the house that I had left behind. Even in the dream, the walls were pale green, the shutters dark, and the golden light filled that room also. I wanted to go to him. I wanted Michael to see me, but he didn't. He couldn't see me or hear my voice. He was sitting on the bed, speaking to someone on the telephone, speaking to Mara, left behind in the other room with golden light. I stood in the doorway while he told her that they had gone through all my letters and papers and journals. All my letters . . . they had found nothing. His voice was confidential. I heard him tell her, "It doesn't make any sense. Why would anyone want to do this?"

Then Mara came down the hallway, past me, and into the room. I wanted them to see me. I wanted to show them I was still alive, but they didn't see me. They just kept talking as though I weren't there.

"I can't see how anyone could want to do it . . . how anyone could want to die."

I wasn't dead. My head began to hurt, watching them, a pressure in my head and chest like rage or crying. I came forward then, toward them, in my dream.

"Can't you," I whispered, "can't you see?"

But what had started so softly began to grow until I was screaming at them, and they were frozen, staring, finally seeing me, but they were afraid.

"Do you really want to know?" I screamed again.

And then I took a conspiratorial tone, smiled, and said softly, "I can tell you if you really want to know."

Before I could go on, my mother appeared at the end of the hall. She came down the hallway, like everything else in the dream, but she was coming toward me, watching me. They were all watching me, and she turned, everything happening so slowly. She was angry. She turned to face me, her eyes a pure black with something shining, lights shining in the irises of her eyes. Her body was dark and roiling, like smoke, and she fell on me. She was burning, her body burning, but in flames that were black, black feathers like wings above her black body. And her face and head were a mask—black eyes, a black hood, an ivory black beak. I felt her on me, her whole body burning. I felt her wings beating the frame of my body, smashing my skull and chest, clawing my eyes, tearing the skin of my face with her talons. I was pleading with her not to hurt my eyes. I covered my head with my arms, and I felt her beak tear at the flesh of my knees, at my thighs, and the tenderest flesh, the secret flesh like a perfect seashell in shreds then. I was bleeding and I tried to pull at her claws, but they wouldn't come away. I couldn't pull her away and her wings were still beating a wind that was burning like fire all around me. I was screaming; I screamed over and over till I awoke.

I couldn't remember where the sound had come from at first. I couldn't tell where the choking sound had come from, but when I woke up, I was at the bottom of the sea.

In the darkness that had submerged my bed, a small white shark was swimming. It circled, coming closer, and moved through an arc of green phosphorescent light, pale; disappeared into the darkness; turned, its tail pulling swiftly side to side, an effortless, visceral beating. It circled back again, homing closer and closer to me in the dark—a shadow that glowed and darkened then suddenly disappeared.

At the side of my bed a kitten was crying, plaintive, afraid. She was hardly real, her white fur shining a deathly color in the light that spilt across the floor from the alarm clock beside the bed. She paced, knocking gently with her forehead against the edge of the cover that was hanging down to the floor. I pushed myself up to sit at the edge of the bed. I reached out and caught hold of her. I gathered her up, her tiny body weightless in my hands, and pressed her to my neck. I was awake now. But in the darkness, numbly, I felt the wetness on my cheeks, my eyes. The terror of my dreams would subside, I knew. The ghosts of my life of a decade ago would begin to dissolve. But he would still be there in the water, his eyes, his body in pieces.

Part I

Part I

1

The Morning After

When I'd gotten back across the bay that first windy morning, after the salon, I had a message waiting. Kelley had called— there was something she wanted to tell me. Could I come over?

I went to her door at the back of the little duplex we had shared since my graduation the summer before. We always used our doors on the side, by the driveway. They each led into a kitchen. The morning was sunny, and I remember standing in the doorway of the room beyond, waiting to let my eyes adjust to the dark. The curtains were closed, and no fire was left on the hearth. She wanted to tell me that he had come by the night before. I knew she meant Aiden. It was a Friday night. I imagined him coming across the bay after work to spend the evening with her, but I'd been gone and hadn't seen him. She'd told him she wanted to go back to Sean, and he had left without saying anything. He had met his father for a drink somewhere that same night, but no one had seen him since. She was worried.

The next morning Kelley called again and told me she had had a dream the night before. In the dream she saw him lying somewhere near water; she thought he was still alive, somewhere near the bay. That was all she could see, just the water in drops against his skin.

She asked me to drive her to the hills beyond the Headlands near the little valley on the northern side of the Gate. He went running there sometimes. Maybe he'd fallen and was badly hurt, unable to get help. We might find where he had parked. But she wasn't sure where the trail started, and I could show her.

The First Dream

In the first night after his death, I had the visitation dream, so vivid, as though he had really come to me. It was the night after Kelley had told me he was missing, before we knew yet what had happened.

In the dream, I'm wandering in one of the old houses on Oxford Street by the university, in Fraternity Row. There are so many other young people like me there; it's like a big party. I'm trying to find my way somewhere; I'm making my way toward the staircase landing (to leave?) from upstairs, when I see Aiden coming toward me along a hallway. He's naked above the waist, wearing only a big white towel wrapped around his waist as though he's just come out of the shower, and his hair is wet and his face—just as he looked on the night I'd first met him, standing in the rain. He's dripping with water. He moves toward me with that expression, the look in his eyes I remember seeing when he was with Kelley—like a puppy, so giddy. He hugs me. He tells me he has been looking everywhere for me.

All the while I'm feeling a growing confusion and panic . . . the way you might feel if you woke up one morning and walked out the door of your house and no one recognized you as yourself, and everyone you met called you, instead, by someone else's name and treated you as though you were that other person.

In the dream, I can't speak, but I keep thinking: This is a mistake; he doesn't see who I am.

I hear the words forming in my head over and over: "I'm not Kelley, I'm not Kelley . . . !"

I try to tell Aiden, but they won't come out. I can't speak; I just keep feeling the words inside me. And finally, almost like a cry, I tell him, "You've got to find Kelley, you have to find her!"

But just as I can say them, as though he senses what's coming, he leaves me, disappears, as though I've somehow hurt him. I wake up and he is gone.

Sofie

Sofie had been a fashion model in her youth. Sitting across from me on an ottoman in the living room of Juliette's house, she still looked glamorous in her soft pink knit suit and silk stockings, her hair done up in soft curls. She had survived cancer only a few years before and she was still beautiful. Her son Sean had inherited the softness of his dark eyes from her, the curve of his lips, and a darker, thicker version of her curls.

I want to remember it as a day in spring or early fall, because the room was filled with light, her dress was light, the sun was out. But it must have been closer to midwinter, because Sofie turned and looked at me intently and asked me a question that caught me completely off guard.

"Darien," she said, "do you think there is any hope of Sean and Kelley getting back together?"

I could tell how much it had been weighing on her that they were apart; she was worried for Sean. I had to cast about mentally for a moment before understanding why she believed I could answer. Someone must have told her that Kelley and I were friends.

But her question disarmed me, and I answered from my heart, from someplace secret even to myself. I answered what I wished for them then, what I wished for myself: some bond that could not be broken. I looked down for barely a moment to search that secret place before saying, "I can't imagine the two of them not together."

I remember it seemed to comfort her, but I don't want to believe that was the reason I'd said it. I don't want to believe it mattered in what happened later. I would not remember our conversation again until years later, when I thought back upon Sofie and what she had wanted for her son, and about the late afternoons that winter before Aiden died, when Sean began coming by again to see Kelley while she was alone at the house. I knew he had never meant to lose her, even less for it to turn out that way.

Everything happened too quickly at the time for anyone to put the possibilities together, events rushing past like a current to the sea, carrying them along just on the surface, perfectly unprepared.

The Driveway

Aiden and Kelley had met through close friends at a party that October, sometime near Halloween. The first time I saw them together was a rainy night a few days later. I had just emerged from the house to go out for the evening. They were arriving, and we passed one another in the narrow drive on the side of the house, to go through the familiar drill of rearranging the cars. They were all together—Aiden and his best friend, Kelley and hers.

I stood to one side to let them pass, and even though there were four of them, I remember only Aiden and Kelley, and I only remember her smiling her sweet smile for a moment before looking down, and I glanced intently at him and was introduced. I remember him smiling broadly; he seemed giddy with happiness accompanied by his friends. They made some invitation, which I declined.

There is this puzzle in my memory. Even though we were all standing in the rain, only Aiden made no attempt to avoid becoming drenched. Afterward I would remember his face turning to smile at me and the water in drops against his skin, almost as though he were standing under a separate sky, and noticing how he didn't seem to mind.

The Snapshot

I remembered one afternoon hearing a knock at the back door. When I opened the door, Aiden was standing there with that funny crooked grin he had when he was joking around.

"C'mon and be in our family portrait." He pointed to everyone standing at the end of the driveway in the afternoon sun.

"I can't," I said.

I hated having my picture taken, which he knew from previous occasions. I squinted, trying to make out the strange faces, all of which were turned toward me.

Everything seemed very silly suddenly. "I can't even walk over there," I said flatly, pleased with myself for being difficult with him.

"I don't have my contacts," I offered then, out of politeness.

He had turned to go back to his friends, but when he realized I wouldn't follow him, he came back up behind me on the steps and put his arms around me, turning us toward the camera, which Kelley held and snapped. He was as straightforward as a child—wanting to do something but not entirely sure of himself or me, as though I might bolt away completely, like a frightened colt. But I didn't. I was taken off guard, and I stood perfectly still.

"C'mon, Darien," I remember him saying softly in my ear. "Maybe this'll be the one."

The Broken Bird

Her father had left their family when Kelley was a little girl. Of his three children, she was the only one who refused, for nearly two decades, to speak to him. Her mother remarried, but she and her husband were killed when the children were still young. Kelley had been close to her grandmother, who was the center of their family from that time onward. The winter that she met Aiden, her grandmother was dying. Kelley spent nights in Marin, nursing her through the last part of her life.

Aiden had been with her at the funeral, and Sean had gone also. It was held in a beautiful craftsman's church in Ross, but Kelley told me that at some point in the middle of the service, a transient person came through the doorway carrying a large portable stereo, blasting the music into the church. Everyone was jarred and shaken, and Sean quickly stood up from his place and pulled the man outside.

We used to smile at Kelley's stoic self-description in the weeks afterward: she wasn't depressed; she just wanted to sleep a lot. After the night her grandmother died in her arms, she became even better at drifting off. She could fall asleep almost in the middle of a conversation, sitting beside you in a theater or in the half a minute you might be out of the room. This was funny to me at the time, but one day I would learn what that was like: sleep as the coveted "comforter," like some magical drug with no side effects that you begin to crave.

One night we'd had dinner together, and Aiden and I were clearing the dishes when one of us noticed Kelley had fallen asleep on the couch. She lay exactly where she'd been when he'd gotten up. We were surprised; hardly a moment had passed. He went to get a blanket and I watched as he covered her. Seeing them, my throat hurt suddenly—his tenderness for her, like a child with a broken bird, so deep as not to be contained by the room around them. I left then, but she called me later, the next morning, and said that she'd woken up in her room ("he must have carried me asleep in his arms"), but she couldn't remember.

The Elms

It's like this when you survive. You will remember a morning, suddenly. You are still marking time by counting the days and then the weeks since he has gone. It was the day the three of you came to this same place together, to run the track above the school. You were locking the car, then following behind them up the sidewalk lined with elm trees, to the gate of the park. You looked up the hill at him. He was being funny, doing things to make the two of you laugh: silly things, hugging the trees as though they were people, teasing her, clowning. It was sunny that day. Deep purple and scarlet leaves were scattered along the sidewalk, the air crisp and cool, and thick white clouds in a blue sky.

You will remember that morning when you return later. Then it will be different. You'll be alone. The sky will be clouded over, but still the day will be beautiful. There will be a sparkling, powerful wind, and sometimes it will rain in short, scattered bursts and a sprinkling of heavy drops. You will have run longer than you usually do. When finally you stop, you want just to stay there, still, looking at the sky, the clouds, and the ragged part of their cover where the bright white of the sun is breaking through.

You lie down on a bench, your eyes closed, just to feel your body in the exquisite peacefulness of having been forcibly fatigued. The wind is playing around you; you open your eyes to watch it rush through the leaves of a plum tree that arcs above you, beside the path where the bench stands.

It starts to sprinkle again, faintly, the drops making tiny spectrums of color on the leaves, and the air and the whiteness of the clouds moving fast above. That's when you will think of him. You want him to come back. It is so beautiful under those clouds with the wind rushing—a place that will never exist for him again. You hear the word *never* until it becomes a silent deep sinking in your own body, a wordless pleading with the sky and the water and that bridge.

You sit up suddenly. You run back down the sidewalk to the car, the people passing by staring at you, at your face shining with a salty wetness that has not come from the rain.

2

The View of San Quentin and Mt. Tam

December 1990

Whenever I cross from the northeastern side, with the water below me and the tiny islands, I see the Sleeping Lady and the spare walls of the prison at her feet, poised at the edge of the bay, and I think of you. And sometimes I almost feel you there beside me. And always you are smiling, and always I feel loved, as though you are trying to tell me, through her beautiful shape in the distance and the shining of the clouds, that you're okay, trying to tell me not to be afraid and never to let go.

> *I long to invoke the shining colors of your white dance, and*
> *you are silent . . .*
> *Are you still at the bottom of the bay?*
> *Or was it different, not the end of something moving?*
> *How I long to see you, long for someone who has seen the*
> *shapes of that long descent, the lure of jewel lights in the*
> *water, the view from the bridge before falling.*

Part II

3

Arcadia

July 1971

I dreamt that they had brought me back home. I was eleven then. Asleep in the night, in the house by the ocean, where Mara had taken me to be safe, I dreamt that they had found me and brought me back. It was summertime, just like in the real time. Only in the dream it was daylight. I was at home again, in the garden at the back of the house. I could see the dark shingles of the roof, the glass doors, wide and shining, and the baskets that hung from the eaves where the hummingbirds built their nests.

Everyone was there, inside. I knew that my mother was there too, and I was alone in the garden. In the dream I saw my body. I was wearing shorts because it was so hot. I was barefoot, and my feet were brown from the summer sun. Before long, night would have come.

In the dream I knew that everything was the way it had always been, the way it would be on that day, and in the night, too. And it would be the same way after the night was finally over, when I woke up again in the morning.

This is how I knew what it felt like to be a prisoner, watching the water through the iron bars of a window in a cell, watching the sea blinking and shining in the sun, rippling, and curling toward the sand in the wind, watching with such longing you forget that the walls still surround you. It was a nightmare turned inside out. In the dream, I wanted to go back. I longed to go back to the place where I'd fallen asleep, where I was free. But the house by the ocean wasn't real anymore. The garden was real, and the house where I was born. In my dream there was no way out of my world.

Do you know how sometimes, if you listen carefully, you can hear the clicking of crickets even though it isn't night? They wake up sometimes in the day, suddenly, by accident, and creak once or twice into the silence and the heat, but only if you're holding very still and standing by a place where they are sleeping in the sun. You can hear them if you wait, perfectly still and quiet, soundless, and they will forget themselves. I heard one single cricket in my dream "click" into the afternoon in the garden and stop.

I had the feeling that someone was watching me—not a person, but God. That He was there inside my head, inside my brain, and He could see me, my thoughts and my eyes watching things: my body, slender in my pale shorts, my feet bare in the summer heat. I held very still, afraid. We were alone inside of me, and it was like being in a dark house with a shadow, in a room so black with darkness that you can't see your hands before you. The door is locked from the outside, and there is only emptiness and a shadow you can feel around you.

I had the feeling that we were playing a game together. Only it wasn't innocent anymore and I was losing. I held still, and my body felt hollow like a shell curving around emptiness. And somehow nothing else mattered in the world, even to God, except for what was happening between us. The people in the house didn't matter. They were a part of the game, like pieces on a chessboard. The garden itself was one of the pieces. The summer was a piece too, and the heat. But I was real, and God was real. He was playing against me. We were playing, and I was losing, and He waited—watching me.

I knew I could not make the game stop. And I wondered what would happen to me when it was over.

Then in the dream I saw Mara. I saw her through the glass doors that led into an alcove behind the entry hall on the other side of the glass. And in the dream, I watched while she ran to the door of the house that led to the driveway, and she pulled at the handle. She pulled at the door on the other side of the glass, but my mother had followed her. Mara was trying to get out, and my mother grabbed at her arm.

I tried to get through the glass door. I didn't want her to leave me. I pulled at the glass door, but it wouldn't open. The door had been locked from the inside. I could see the reflections of the huge trees behind me in the garden. I pulled at the door, and the reflections trembled and splintered and stilled again, untouched except for the barest movement of leaves stirred by a breeze.

I called through the glass, but no one saw or heard me; Mara couldn't see me or hear my voice. I wanted her to take me with her. She said something to my mother and wrenched her arm free all at once. While I stood watching, unnoticed by them, Mara undid the latch at the top of the door, ran out of the house and across the drive to her car and drove away.

After she was gone, I could still see the trees and the drive through the glass and the door that she had left open on the other side. I stood with my hand on the glass and watched the reflection of what was behind me, and later, when I looked up again, the door on the other side had been closed and no one was there.

4

The Evil Night

August 1973

Watching her was like being in a dream, like the dreams that come back again and again in which there is water everywhere and I am losing consciousness, my eyes cannot open, I cannot breathe or escape, my body floating in the shallows of shadowy green water.

But she never knew that it was like that for me, and she would let the room just fill up around her: things that had happened, things she had seen and heard, words that had been spoken to her years ago crowding in again, all suddenly more real than we were then. All at once we would be gone and there would be only the spell that she was under. I wanted to get away, but I was afraid to leave her and there was nowhere to go, and even if there had been, it would be worse to come back later and find whatever she had done while she was alone.

One time, it was summer, with the perfect, heavy stillness of the earth cooling in the dusk. Outside, through the long glass doors, the darkness was coming; the crickets had begun their soft chanting. That night I had just turned thirteen, so I stayed, not to leave her there alone, because I was no longer a child.

I watched her from the doorway. I knew it had begun. Something had started her again. I had been gone all day; she was angry about that. I thought she would come back to me, but she didn't. She could see things that I could not, but I could feel them, the rushing of silent voices all around her body, the press of their shadows filling the room, and I could feel the terror of her descent, darker than the vertigo of sleep, down a well that had no bottom, a tunnel that she made in falling. I saw her in that room before me, but that's not really where we were.

She began to tear at herself, at her face, her skin. She tore at her clothes and pulled them away. She seemed to know I was still there with her, beneath those voices. I wanted to go then, I wanted to leave her, but I could not move. She took everything in the room, all the furniture that she could lift, and turned it upside down.

She said they buried their children, the bodies of their unborn, torn from their wombs before their term, that they came back to dig them up over and over again.

Remembering now, I think of that little blue book all children see when they are first starting out learning to read. A blue cover with yellow letters and the story of a little bird who's fallen from the nest, a huge bulldozer moving earth everywhere and the little bird's constant question, while he searches everywhere, trying to remember what she looked like. This is the question I want to ask: Are you my mother . . . ?

"Who, mom, who?"

Whimpering, tearing at herself, she said, "Digging like dogs with their bones . . . lust like the lust of dogs, so strong they would lie in the dirt, lie with dogs in their excrement, fucking in the dirt!"

"*Who a*re you talking about . . . ?" I asked her, starting to cry.

And a pause as though searching to see their faces in her mind . . . as if she could see them before her even then, "The devil worshippers," she said.

She'd pulled open the glass doors, gone into the yard, and come back naked, carrying earth in her hands. She did something then, while I watched her from the little corridor, and it burned to see it, the way blinding burns inside your eyes. And the suddenness made everything else disappear, the room and all the other sounds of the night disappearing. Only the sound of her voice, screaming and crying, the dirt covering her body and face, spilling from her hands and from the secret folded place she'd once told me was sacred, the mud falling down her thighs.

It made everything stop. My eyes were open. They stayed open the way a cat's do when he freezes in the dark with the headlights of the car shining on him. Only a cat is blind that way, but I was not blind. She did this to herself while I stood watching, and everywhere the air was pulling away from me, and the whiteness of my own brain came in very close, enfolding me. I felt something covering me, covering all of my body, that started in a tingling at the top of my head and became a suffocating, scalding thing. I had the sensation that I was falling, the center of my body dropping, and I bent over to hold myself at the sinking place. I heard the sound of someone crying, and it came from the place inside me that I was trying to hold.

Then someone near me, the touch of a hand, pulling me up. My brother Ian, there behind me. I could see his eyes and in them the lightness at the top of his head, the same whiteness behind his eyes like the whiteness I had seen in the horses' eyes when they rear and bolt, the whiteness of fear in all animals, while he pulled on me to come away from her, never taking his eyes from her.

In the morning when I woke up, the house was quiet. I knew I was alone except for her, sleeping somewhere. I was calm: my body, everything beneath my skin, filled with emptiness.

Ian had left in the night to go back to the dorms. Mara had come for him in her car after visiting friends, and together they would make the long drive back down to the university. He was listening for her and slipped out without my mother hearing them, and together they'd gone away.

I was late for school, but I still wanted to go. I lay in my bed and thought first I would try to see her: I would go into her room. I knew she was alone and maybe she would just be sleeping.

I dressed and went to her door, and then I heard her call my name. Her voice was soft and sweet, like a young girl's. When I came into the room she was lying in her bed. She said my name softly and sat up in bed and held out her hand. And I went to the edge and sat down beside her, folding the pleats of my school skirt beneath me, which she had taught me to iron so carefully. I could feel her eyes watching my own, watching my face. She held out her hand and I took it in my own. Her hands were strong and beautiful. The fingers were long and slender and tapered, but they weren't delicate because she was tall, and her bones weren't small enough to be delicate. The way they were was even more beautiful, and mine would be like them someday.

She told me she was sorry, her voice soft.

"I'm sorry," she said. There was nothing to say; I couldn't speak anyway. Then she asked, "What happened?"

I looked up at her finally. I tried to make my voice even.

"Can't you remember?" I asked her. And I became invisible to her again, for a moment. She didn't see me or the room any longer or our hands holding together. Her eyes searched a line at the edge of the bed, motionless, turned inward, seeing . . . nothing? I could tell she was afraid. And I knew suddenly that she'd seen her body, what she had done. I knew she'd woken up in the middle of the night, while I lay in an exhausted sleep, and she'd gone to the room we had been in before and everything had lain just as it was.

I was sorry. I felt sorry I'd asked that question.

Suddenly I wanted her not to know. I wished I had done something before this moment, quickly. I wanted to wash her body, to carry her to the bathroom and bathe her, to make everything be the way it was before, to wash her before she knew, before we both could remember. But it wouldn't have mattered by then anyway.

I wanted to whisper that nothing had happened, all the memories that would come back again another night, to tell her none of it had ever happened. I wanted to be the one she could believe and to say, "It's just this one moment, now. This is the beginning." But it was too late.

Later, while she was dying, I thought sometimes about that morning, about what it would be like for me when she was gone. I wondered if I would not sometimes forget and want to go to her, to hold her hands in my own and watch them as I'd done before, when I had learned to see them perfectly.

After awhile I left her. I wanted to go to school. I was dressed, but a light rain was falling. I walked out into the morning, down the long block to the corner where I had spent so many other mornings when I was little, waiting for the bus. I walked past the other houses, some of them mansions with wide, peaceful lawns in front and gardens and arbors with brick pillars, and gates. I walked around the curve of the street up the hill toward the end, where it stopped at the old cemetery at the foot of the hills. I passed a long space filled with ivy, where a wall surrounded a house. I glanced down, trying to keep the rain, which had grown heavier, off my face. At the side of the road, thrown down against the dark leaves, lay the body of a cat—dark gray with striped fur matted from the rain and from its own blood, its head mangled and wet. I stopped, looking down at it without knowing what to do. I thought it might have died in the night or in the early morning. I felt unspeakably weary, and finally I walked on.

Another summer, ten years before, my oldest brother had come running home all the long way I was now walking, because riding in the bus on his way to school, he'd seen our cat, dead and lying by the side of the road. I was too young then to have gone with him, only three or so. But he'd run all the way back the three miles from school and come to my mother and told her and run out again into the street. I'd heard what he'd said, and she'd taken me in her arms to comfort me and followed him. I was hysterical over the cat, and she stood holding me at the end of our driveway,

with the neighbors staring down the street where the cat lay somewhere. But she couldn't go to look; she didn't want me to see. She
went to collect the mail from the box at the curb. We had received
butterflies that a company used to send in the mail as gifts, pressed
against cards and wrapped in cellophane, and we'd keep them to
mark our place in picture books. She held the butterflies up for me
to see, smiling, hoping to comfort me. "Look what they've sent,"
she said. "Look at the butterflies. They'll be your pets now."

5

Laces

Spring 1963

I sit sidesaddle in the new white chair at one side of my room. My mother kneels before me. She is singing a soft, singsong nursery song, "Once a Little Daisy," "This Little Piggy," or "How Much Is That Doggy in the Window?" She takes my foot in her hands, pulls my stocking on.

She talks to me in baby talk in between phrases of the song. I know she's happy. I watch her hands, her fingers, their long tapering, the place on her thumb where the sewing needle from the machine went through, leaving a thick white line. She props my stockinged foot on her thigh and reaches for my shoe on the floor beside her. The material of her pants is stretched tight across her thighs where she's rested my foot as she kneels.

My shoes are small white leather Buster Brown lace-ups. She always carefully loosens the laces on both sides, all the way down. The shoes get polished with chalky white polish where they're scuffed, but the laces are mottled white and gray. She wiggles my foot into the shoe, singing, and does the laces back up, going the opposite way.

I love watching her. It's always the same, so fast, her beautiful hands. I watch her but can never figure it out.

6

The Police

September 1974

She calls the police. She calls the police on herself, or on him? He's hurting her. He wants something (money? car keys?); she's not forthcoming. She calls the police and tells them she wants to be taken away. She knows there's a state hospital in Camarillo—a psych hospital. She worked in a state hospital once—in Warm Springs. She knows what it means. She knows something's wrong. If her own son can hurt her like this, something must be wrong with her. She's decided maybe that's where she belongs. She hasn't been drinking this time. She seems perfectly lucid. She tells the dispatcher she wants them to take her there.

The police will come, but they won't take her there. I don't know what they'll do, but I know they won't do that. I don't want to be there when they arrive. My brother will tell them nothing is wrong. Mara and Ian are gone, away at college. It's just us three; my father is away at work. I don't want to talk to the police; I don't want to stand in the hallway with my mother and my brother and the police. They will come into the house, and it will feel like so much more than two men entering a room. They will be tall, or the darkness of their uniforms will make them seem tall, will take up an enormous space. It will be hard to breathe with them there—the sound of their radio, the sight of their guns will trigger something frightening. They will stand, watching us warily, tight-lipped, waiting for something explosive to occur at any moment. They will not even attempt to mediate between my mother and my brother. They will just be thinking of how to get out of the situation alive.

I don't want to see them. I especially don't want to break down in front of them, at the sight of the uniformed men in that entryway. I want nothing to do with this; I want to skip this piece.

I dress to leave the house. I call my teacher. She's a friend, a private music teacher, not from school.

"The police are coming to the house," I tell her. "Can I stay with you tonight?"

I've never called her before. She sounds confused and even more panicked than I am.

"I'm teaching right now," she says. She covers the phone.

She'll send her student. He'll leave right away. Still, it will be about half an hour before he can get there.

"I'll wait outside," I say.

The police arrive before I can leave. It's just like I'd thought it would be: they're all standing in the front hall. (They've not been offered a seat or anything to drink.)

I want to help her, but I can't.

They look up at me as I come down the hallway.

"Who's this?" they ask, watching me.

"Her daughter," I say.

I move past them to get to the door.

"Where are *you* going?" one of them asks.

"Out." I can barely manage to say this word.

For once, no one says anything.

I leave and walk to the end of the drive. I wait there in the darkness. Finally, the ride comes. He pulls over, gets out, and comes across to open the door for me. He is older and very polite.

He nods at the police car parked outside the drive. They did not pull in.

"Looks like you've got some trouble tonight . . ."

"Yes." I nod. And we are silent for the rest of the way.

Kyle

I got caught somehow in the middle, between them. I was younger; how could I know how it began? Something went wrong between them so much earlier than I can remember.

Later, she would be trying to protect me, or sometimes I would be trying to protect her. It was a "no contest" effort, completely impossible to win. He was invincible.

Some years later I sit in a therapist's office.

He asks me, "What exactly was it that happened? Can you be more specific?"

I've made some allusion to my brother's violence. I've given a kind of verbal flowchart of its direction, the hierarchy in his choice of "victims," or "objects of his wrath." He could choose my mother or me and sometimes but less often my older brother, but he would never touch my older sister or our father—obviously. How was this allowed to happen?

When I'm asked this question, asked to describe what I witnessed or endured, my mind goes completely blank. I could remember if I were alone, but in that office on that day, I look down at the floor, at my hands. I'm embarrassed. I literally cannot think, let alone speak.

The doctor looks at me. He studies me. I tell him I don't know; I don't remember.

But he knows that I do, that sometimes I can remember, just not in front of anyone else, not to give that picture to anyone else. I realize then that this is the thing over which I feel the most shame, the one thing in a complex tangle of stranger and more horrible things that I can't bear describing to anyone else.

The doctor says in a quiet voice, "You've blocked it out . . . It's too painful and you've blocked it out."

I repeat this story to my oldest brother. He laughs. I'm not sure why he laughs. It becomes our joke for years afterward, a catch-phrase we throw at one another in other contexts, anytime we have a lapse of memory:

"It's too painful." We smile. "You blocked it out."

I don't know what made him different. He had a comfort with violence that the rest of us did not acquire, though we might have suffered more than he did, physically at least. I realize now: he didn't even need to be angry. He only needed to be thwarted in something, anything, even something inconsequential. Then he used force to get through. No lead time. Just one moment and then the next: desire, frustration, rage. I was told that as a child, a toddler, he'd been so different—so sweet, so anxious to please others, to share whatever he had. I don't know what changed in him, but I know it happened silently, secretly, without any of us seeing where it was heading until it was too late. He was already there, already that way—uncontrollable.

7

The Closet

Fall 1974

I am in the closet in my room at the end of the hall. My back is braced against the narrowest wall, to the left of the door, in the farthest corner, a wall that spans the depth of the space. There are two walls on either side of me also, so close that nothing can fit between these walls and my body. I am surrounded by immovable barriers, except for the side I'm facing, where I can see part of the opposite wall and, to my right, the place where the door is. I am fourteen years old. Twenty years later, I'll learn that finding a small space like this is what they tell children to do.

But moments before, I was not here. I'm only here now because I was walking down the hallway past the door to my youngest brother's room. Hearing him say or do something, I let fall a casual remark, almost under my breath but loud enough for him to hear, something sarcastic. In response to what? I can't even remember.

I am in the closet crouching down holding my head, folding my arms with my elbows bent across the top of my skull, pushing down as hard as I can against the pressure inside, and later, with my face buried in my hands; because, hearing my remark, he's come out of his room, and without hesitating in his rush, he's picked me up, sweeping my legs out from under me, like the men in the movies do, carrying women across a threshold. But I've gotten taller now for my age, and he has to jockey to get my body into the position he wants, almost parallel to the floor, so that when I fall, when he throws me down against the wall and the floor, I'll fall against my back.

I'm in the closet now because whatever pain I would have felt I can't feel, and I can't feel it because the pressure in my head eclipses everything.

I am here because suddenly I'm no longer willing to let him see me cry, as he has so many hundreds of times before. I hate myself for crying, for it hurting, and because now I need a quiet place to hold the flood beating inside me that I am suddenly feeling all at once, like a flutter of moths' wings against the inside of me, the rain of these blows inside my head from those hundreds of other times, like the beating of wings against a screen that stands between a hundred tiny, frantic creatures and a light.

I am crouching there with my back braced against the wall because I can't think any longer well enough to watch from everywhere, and I need darkness and a place that is small and enclosed from which to see if he should follow, if he comes through the door looking for me, someplace where I'll have the leverage of something behind me that's safe, something to keep my balance against, not to worry about falling, so that before he can try to pull me up by my arms or my hair or grab me from someplace that won't be from behind, before anyone can get that close to me, before he can get to my body, I'll see him and I'll be able to kick, several times, hard, first at his knees and then over and over again at whatever part of his body is closest to me when he hits the floor.

Because I have never felt this way before. Because I have never thought this before, and I'm frightened. I know suddenly that in not much longer a time one of us is going to hurt the other very badly. Either he is going to hurt me badly by accident, or I am going to hurt him, on purpose, to keep him from hurting me again. Or I am going to kill myself to keep myself from killing him.

I have lost something. I'm not like myself anymore; I'm like them, and I'm afraid in a little while I will be doing to one of them what they have been doing to me, to save myself. Because I'm waiting for this feeling to ebb away, this pressure, and beneath it, a well of rage, a perfect path of will so strong it won't require thought any longer or means, just an opportunity when one day, through the simple glimmer of my will, I'll follow a perfect unbroken path and one of us will "end." Because I want one of us to die.

Because I'm waiting, now, with my back against the wall, for this knowledge—the certainty of my will and the means to ebb away, waiting to recognize myself again. Because now they have won.

I am in the closet, and he never comes. But there is, inside me, the path of my will, the perfect field from my will to an end, and I know all of this now, except how short a time will pass before I choose.

8

Golden Gate

1979

*I*n my dream I can fly.
   I start from somewhere above the hills on the northern side of the bay. I can see the mouth of the bay and the place where the Gate would be, the two points of land curving back along the Pacific and the Headlands. The colors of everything are deep and vibrant, like the colors of the jewel shapes in a kaleidoscope: the brilliant azure blue of the sky, yellow-orange hills, like the orange of a desert mesa. The water—endless layers of a perfect, pale fluid over sand at the bottom of the bay, warm and salty and empty.

   There is no bridge, there are no people, and no evidence that they will ever arrive, and nothing is green. The world is young. Only a perfect stillness, a seamless waiting that will continue for eons in a brilliant sun.

   And all I am is my eyes.

   I soar down along the sides of the bowl made by the hills, in long dives to just above the surface of the water. I have no body except the energy I use to keep myself in flight. The sight of this once familiar place in this state beyond imagination fills me with an uncontainable gladness and relief; it was this way once, and one day it will be like this again.

The world is young, primordial, with perfect clarity; nothing has yet happened that cannot be undone.

I want to be like this again.

9

Turning

1974

I don't remember when, exactly, I "turned the corner" where it became impossible to think of the future anymore. I had no awareness of myself except through the eyes of those who were closest to me then. Their words and gestures and expressions make up the only memories I have about myself from that time, apart from the dreams.

Later, looking back, trying to retrace my steps to that point, I thought often of a night in the fall when Mara was home visiting, and we were together again in the room we'd shared for so many years. I was fourteen and Mara was twenty-one. I was lying in my bed, and she lay across from me in hers, surrounded by papers. We'd spent the day together at a library downtown, an old granite building with separate wings and floors connected by the old, narrow stairways. Somewhere in the stacks I'd found a set of books about a family of several sisters growing up in the late nineteenth century. On the cover of one volume was a picture that showed the girls gathered together around a gaming table in a parlor. They were wearing long dresses, velvety moss-green and garnet colors, with wide skirts and high, narrow collars and cuffs. Their hands were delicate. I sat down to read two or three of the books while Mara studied her nursing texts, and we stayed there until it began to get dark.

Later that night, lying in bed, I thought about sleep. I imagined the house in darkness and the night slipping by while I lay in another world, and then I thought about waking up again in the morning and beginning all over again. I realized that I dreaded it happening anymore. It had begun to feel like a mistake. I said something out loud, softly, talking half to myself and to Mara at the same time. I told her I didn't want to go to school. I know it wasn't the words themselves but something in my voice that made her stop and put down what she was writing. She stared at me with a blank kind of alarm that I have not forgotten. I felt confused. I was unspeakably tired without wanting to sleep.

Later Mara said it was a combination of factors that made her realize it could not go on. Something a doctor had said, a colleague of my father's, had frightened them, my father and Mara. I'd undergone some recent tests to diagnose [newly] emerging problems with my vision. One of his colleagues told my father to get some other kind of help for me. The doctors couldn't understand what was happening, they couldn't find a cause, except perhaps stress. Was everything okay at home?

But we didn't tell them.

I had begun having episodes of a kind of temporary blindness; they were physical episodes that came with increasing frequency in that year. My father had brought me to the medical center for tests, and his colleagues had brought specialists in, but no one could find a cause. The episodes came intermittently, across the left eye, the eye I sighted with, and it was like trying to see through a silver shimmering film, little explosions of light sparkling everywhere on the inside of my eye, a silver phosphorescent shining that gradually obscured everything so that if I blinked my right eye shut, I could see nothing at all. Looking into my eyes, no one else could see anything unusual from the outside. The blindness would last about fifteen minutes at a time, then slowly begin to disappear again, not all at once but gradually, starting at one side and lifting away, like breath from a cold window.

In the last visit I remember being alone with my father and one other doctor, a neurologist, in the examining room. I remember her asking me if anything was causing me fear or stress. I shrugged, a little confused by her question. I didn't see her connection. I don't remember who else was there. Finally, I shook my head no.

We went home. I remember that last ride back from the medical center beside my father in the car, how odd it was to be alone with him then. My exhaustion made me at ease. He seemed bewildered and quiet. I thought about all the trouble he had gone to, leaving his own work at the center and his patients, which was so rare for him, and driving me back from the city afterward so I could finish the afternoon at school. He seemed at such a loss that I felt sorry for him. He said something to me, something quiet and unexpected that has completely disappeared from memory.

A few weeks later my mother came alone to pick me up from school for the last time.

She had done something like it one afternoon years before. Mara might have been fifteen, and we were all together in the car, all of us children, on a winter afternoon. My mother had been drinking all day and seemed barely able to make her way along the road, but miraculously she did not attract much attention and we were never stopped, but we were terrified. Mara and I retreated instantly into silence, but my brothers could not contain their rage at being held helplessly captive. The more they complained, the more vindictive she seemed to become, so that, instead of taking the turn to drive us home, she passed it by and headed up toward the hills to the south, about thirty minutes away, the eastern limits of the metropolis. The roads there were narrow, laced between the canyons, sometimes growing into a dirt track carpeted with eucalyptus and rocks. She wound through them for the next hour while we held ourselves motionless against the seats. Slowly it began to grow dark.

The car's speed would change with every fleeting disconnect of her senses so that what she could see of the road, or feel of the car, and her foot on the accelerator, and her ability to steer and all her dwindling attempts to focus became painfully obvious in separate moments.

While the minutes passed, the only force that seemed to be keeping us from going over the side of the cliffs was the effort of keeping perfectly still around each curve, as though our will over our bodies could alter the forces of nature. But afterward I knew it had had nothing to do with us; only the intercession of angels kept us from falling, from going over the edge of the cliffs or from hitting someone else coming toward us head-on. Angelic hands kept everyone else away, angelic wings that enfolded all of us at the precise moments when there was room only for her.

So, when she appeared that day and it began to happen again, I did not want to go on.

This time, she tried to pick someone up—a young boy who was hitchhiking from the all-boys high school down the block. She pulled over when she saw him, and she turned to smile at me. I was so stunned; I could hardly think what was happening. When he got into the car, there was an awkward pause, while she waited for me to react. I looked down into my lap; I felt I would die of shame.

I could only think that she might kill us both.

I said, "Get out of the car; she's drunk." But it was so hard for me to speak, he couldn't hear me.

He said, "What?"

She turned to me in a rage, but I no longer cared what she would do, whether she hit me. I turned halfway in my seat and yelled, "GET OUT OF THE CAR . . . SHE'S DRUNK!"

When he was back on the curb, he stood facing me, and his friend approached and asked what had happened. And he said, "I'll tell you later," and they both stood there watching us. I could see the rage in her face. She was as shocked as I was.

I told her if she didn't take me home right away, I would get out of the car and walk, but I was bluffing. I did not want to pass by the boys now standing and staring at us. I gently moved my hand to the door, as if to open it, before she pulled away from the curb.

I didn't think much about what it would be like; I only remember thinking of Mara and Ian and how important it was to end my helplessness. When we got back home, in the same miraculous way we had so many times before, I went to my room. I changed my clothes. I closed the shutters, but the light still filtered through in narrow shafts. I went to her bathroom, opened her bottle of tranquilizers, and spilled them into my hand. I went to Kyle's bathroom and found the bottle the doctor had given him to calm him, and did the same with his. I also found a bottle of some drug often prescribed for epilepsy that the doctors had prescribed for me to see if it would stop the episodes of temporary blindness in my left eye. They had theorized that the temporary blindness was a kind of epileptic equivalent, though I had never had a seizure or symptoms of any kind. I emptied this bottle into my hand and took those as well. Then I went and lay down.

Kyle came to the door and asked why I had made the room so dark, why was I in bed already? I was tired, I said. And I slept, and I don't remember dreaming anything.

Did she dream or sleep a dreamless sleep, or did she see herself outside her body from above, but only for an instant?

Did she dream or see herself in the bed below, lying peacefully, in the half life? Or did the voices gather around her as she had heard them, felt them rather, gather sometimes before to begin their chant? And were they pulled apart by the channel the angels made to breathe her back? The wishes of others to bring her back, the silent angels that were the thoughts of others that had not yet even been thought or imagined?

Or did they come—the voices or others, the angels—moving like a river, filling the vacuum she'd created, the channel that had opened, through the rent she'd made in the curtain of her life?

All there is in memory are people coming, not just someone coming—that was Mara—but others, not exactly people but spirits, swirling intentions eddying around her, surrounding her, holding her, lightly carrying her with them on the tide of their will to a place different from where she'd been, a place where they wanted her to be—nothing that could be named by words, just a tide of intention, their *intention, something wholly other than her own, free of her own will, something she'd been unable to wish: just to keep living.*

10

The Sidewalk

San Francisco, 1979

All those memories, all the ones begging to be written down, calling for shape or form in an image, a small bit of timelessness, the letters and words on the page can promise: they're all about her and they're either about her hurting herself, while I watch helplessly, or they're about her hurting me.

I dream that I'm at home again, only this time something is different, a wing of the house I have never been in before, an annex with several small rooms, completely new and bare, each behind its single door in a long row down a hallway; and I am in one of those rooms, like a cell, the walls white and smooth and nothing inside, empty except for a phone and the door, and she has locked it to keep me inside. I pick up the phone and my oldest brother, Ian, is there, on the other end; he is in a room near mine. I tell him I'm trapped, the door is locked, but he can't seem to hear me or understand; he can't help me. And I know she's somewhere nearby in a room by herself, waiting—just waiting for the end of this day.

Then suddenly it's over. I'm free. I'm wandering on a street somewhere in a city, alone in the noon light, people around me, going through their day without noticing me or knowing where I've been. I try to orient myself. I walk along trying to remember how I've gotten there, but I can't. I can only remember being back in that room, locked in. I can only remember her, left behind, still alone in that house.

Suddenly it becomes harder and harder for me to walk. I see the narrow squares of the sidewalk in front of me, waiting for me, the long shadows of things behind me, falling against their patience, and reflections in the windows to my right, the warm, shining glass guarding places I will never go. I feel heavy with the knowledge of something I have never seen before, something that feels as old as if it were planted in me at the beginning of my life, the beginning of memory, and I hear the words in my head silently for the first time, over and over.

I try to find my way through the passersby, and to hold myself up, but I can't because suddenly, hearing the words for the first time, my strength fails me, my legs become weak and numb. I can no longer stand up, my throat is hurting, I have to struggle to breathe. Dropping to my knees on the sidewalk, my body folds over on itself. In trying to keep from hurting myself in falling, I lay my forehead gently against the ground.

"You weren't enough . . . you weren't enough . . . she had a choice; you just weren't enough to make her want to . . . stop."

11

Montana

December 1974

Mara came. They asked me where I wanted to go. I wanted to be with a family. I did not want to go to boarding school, with girls I had never met before. I wanted to go back to the ranch where I had spent the summer two years before, with Uncle Evan's family, with my aunt Nina. We had visited every other summer while I was growing up, my mother to see her family, her parents, brother, and sisters.

Sometimes we'd stay in the farmhouse with my uncle, other times in town with my aunts. On the ranch, we spent the mornings with my cousins working in the vegetable garden, picking beans and weeding, before the heat became too intense. Then in the afternoons, we'd wander along the railroad tracks down to the creek or up in the hills. My uncle took us fishing too, sometimes, at cabins up-country. My cousins had their weddings in these summers, and family picnics near the lakes—gatherings we did not have at home in Los Angeles.

My mother had gone back one January, without us, to bury her father. But I had never been to the ranch in winter. That December, after a ride in the dark of early morning through the labyrinthine freeways of Los Angeles, the rain pouring down, Mara navigating, I took a plane from the international airport that landed in the tiny airport in East Helena, where my aunt met me.

It was not a typical winter for Helena yet—milder, with the banks of snow only at the corners of roads and black ice on the creek. In the week left before Christmas vacation, I walked the banks alone in the afternoons, unafraid—a change from how I had always felt as a little girl.

At night, in the farmhouse, I would lie awake alone in the room they had given me, my cousins all sleeping upstairs. I would lie there remembering the stories they'd told in the summers before, of the hobos wandering the train tracks at the boundary of the fields and coming in toward the houses at night. One summer, years before when we were visiting, my brother Ian had been reading Truman Capote's book *In Cold Blood*. He might have been a junior in high school then; I would have been nine or ten. I'd read the title and asked him what it was about and he told us, told me, more than I should have been told: how there were two men and a family that lived too far from town for anyone to hear their screams, how they had tied them to the bed posts and shot them and how afterward they'd had to fill the bodies with gauze to keep the shapes intact for burial. I thought of these things at night, but in the day I did not.

Out on the banks of the creek, hidden from the farmhouse where my aunt was doing her housework, I was not afraid, though we were separated by the hills and ravines and brush. I was not afraid because she had told me I would be safe, and I believed myself to be entirely alone.

I brought a tiny camera with me, an old Instamatic that had been a Christmas gift years before. In the few photographs that survive there is a pale bluish-lavender bruise that was the sky, with huge gray clouds and black earth beside shallow drifts of snow on the creek banks.

Under the leaden sky, the water was even darker than it had been in summer, so dark and so much colder than anything else, than any other place, that it seemed as if the single dark track of water was coming from the place where winter slept. The invisible, unfindable mystery place of cold flowing from there, slowly, became the thick blanket of white and air that almost hurt to breathe, and the gray black ice of later months. It seemed as though all of winter would come ultimately from that stream of dark water, growing out from its sides like the black stain in the cloth covering a wound, the stain of winter growing out from the side of the creek.

Wandering by the creek, I thought of the times before, in summer when we had played there innocently. I tried to find the old trestle we had stood beneath years before, to feel the dizziness of the train going by, hunting for anything moving in the stream, those days when it had been a different world and I had not known what the future held.

But I did not stay. I went back to California two weeks later, not knowing how to transplant myself. I wanted to come home, even though there was no home to return to.

I knew it was no longer a choice. I had become afraid of things I did not understand but knew I could no longer predict. I never forgot that I could not go back home without risking losing my way out again.

A call came just days before I was to leave Helena, from Ian in Los Angeles. He wanted me to know ahead of time, so as not to be hurt or shocked. She was staying in her room; I would see her there. She had completely shaven her head. It was hard for him, he said, to see her that way, and he knew it would be for me too. It was a protest of sorts, against my leaving, something she had done to herself in a fit of helplessness and rage, when she was alone, before anyone could stop her. Mara had not said anything about it to me.

Part III

12

La Honda, California

Halloween 1987

I dream that one day I will tell our child what that special day was like, all the magical things that happened around us. How we woke up by the ocean and watched the waves crash against the rocks and the sand. And drove through that little neighborhood and imagined a house there and our children, what our lives would be like. And later parked above the cliffs by the ocean and slept for a little while. How I bumped my head getting up and tried to wait the right length of time to answer: "Yes, I will. I will marry you," but only managed to say, "Okay."

How a boat had crashed a hole in its side and lay in the shallows, played with by the waves, and the sea otters, wading in the waters just beyond it, watching the spectacle, watching us watching. How the hawk hovered motionless by the car while hunting the grasses there. And the beautiful light, the violet light on the water while we drove back near sunset. And the pumpkins in the fields, and corn. And the little town we drove through, up a narrow street, past a little house with a dog tied in the yard, and a door such a strange and pale color blue with the little screen for their baby.

It seemed that I had spent years of my life watching that water and had come back to have something secret and magical follow us all that day.

Birth Night
Berkeley, California
1989

To My Mother:

How it was, when you were gone—a call came that Sunday morning. Steven was out; I was alone.

It was my father, in Los Angeles. His voice was soft, controlled. He said, "Mom's gone. She died this morning, about ten o'clock."

Remembering the sound of his voice now, I realize how hard he was trying. He couldn't have been worrying about me then, but I heard only gentleness and the sound of his defeat. I was not expecting it.

I was stunned. I said, "I thought you would give me some kind of warning first."

And he said, "We had our warning. Her infection—the pneumonia—was our warning."

"I didn't realize that," I said.

Then there was nothing left to say. Something about when the funeral would be.

It was windy. I remember when Steven came back, I went to the door and stood on the steps with him and told him and the wind was blowing in gusts, through sun and the clouds in the blue sky.

That night something changed, but I didn't know to pay attention until a full twelve hours had gone by, when I realized the strange sensation that had started then, in the night, had become rhythmic. I'd gone into labor without knowing or even being able to pay attention, and all of a sudden I knew what was happening. I called Steven at work that following afternoon. I told him to stay there, though; it would be okay. I thought I had lots of time.

He came home late in the afternoon, and at twilight we began to make our plans to leave for the hospital. Our neighbors and friends had brought flowers and food and their wishes for a safe birth and a little black rubber spider, which we put on top of the bassinet for protection. It was Halloween. At dark we went outside to walk. Little ghosts and goblins wandered by. I don't even remember their faces. I remember the sky: indigo with tiny stars and the still paler gray shadows that had been the brilliant white clouds of the afternoon. That's where you've gone, I told myself. I needed to stop then and stay very still with each contraction. I waited on the sidewalk while Steven held me.

I asked him to take me to the Berkeley Pier. It was late by then, almost twenty-four hours from the beginning. I was stalling for time. We took the car through the dark. The pier was deserted, and the wind had whipped the bay into whitecaps. The road out to the end was rutted, unpaved gravel in places, and every unevenness was almost unbearable through the contractions. I knew it would get even harder if we waited any longer, so we started for the hospital then, along the bay shore with the lights of the city shining across the way, around the curve of the maze and into another river of lights in the darkness from the cars coming across the bridge toward the hills.

They offered me something for pain almost immediately. I remember thinking how odd that was, so soon when we were planning to go on for hours more without it. I refused, not realizing how long it would take. It took until the next morning, through a constant motion of walking, waiting, a limbic listening for messages, like someone deaf and blind trying to interpret vibrations in the darkness surrounding them; only the world I listened for was under my own skin, and the sensations were happening inside myself, behind a barrier I'd never before known: some small part of it that was me and some part of it that was not, and the measure of that difference could not be known, entwined in a way that does not end with a severed cord. I waited, making the world around me still until I could not stay awake any longer and began falling asleep, curled over myself between the pains. I thought of you, the comfort you'd given when I was little and in pain, I called for you silently. I felt only blackness, a perfect complete silence, the absence of you in the world, as though you had disappeared behind those stars and left me completely behind, just before this day when I would need you again.

13

The Voices of the Children

Arcadia 1989

n the voices of the children, I see the canyons that once surrounded us.

While I lie here in near sleep, surrounded by darkness, my own child sleeping at my side, the warmth of the sun on the grass where they play is as real to me as it was those many years ago when I was among them. How, as a child, I had waited sometimes, listening to their laughter from my hidden place where the dust of leaves made a lake for the sunlight pouring down through a screen of branches in broken shafts, a universe of light, tiny stars, and planets spinning in endless motion. How I had lingered there while the voices of the children whom I knew, children I might have played with in the hours or days before, echoed in the still air of the afternoon. In a trance I would watch the errands of the tiny spiders in the brush, their endless delicate machinations.

Now the children have become angels: disembodied, ethereal. They have no faces anymore, their passionate voices making, instead, a picture of the world around them as the noises and rustling of birds and their flight describe the vault of a tower for the man who is blind.

In the darkness of night, I hear the wall of mountains, the stillness of the pool, the silent palm tree and the many ancient oaks, the old carriage house, and the barns. They are standing still as they have done for a hundred years, listening silently to the children who played here before, children whose spirits come back in the dark to this place where they were young.

The house appears in my dreams every night now. Ian says it's the same for him. He sometimes finds himself near the neighborhood but never allows himself to go past the place where it once stood.

It wasn't the house itself but everything around it and everything inside that made it magical: the walls of glass across the back and the long banks of windows in every room at the front, the view of the land and the flower beds and trees from every room; and the sounds of the birds: mourning doves cooing their constant, soft song in the afternoons, woodpeckers, blue jays and crows, and owls sometimes, in the night. And the whisper of the wind in the trees. All the time, behind every memory I hear these sounds.

As a little girl, I'd not wanted to leave to start school. I remembered the solitary afternoons I'd spent as the youngest child still at home, exploring the mysteries of the yard alone, and I did not want to be away. In that place I felt protected from the world.

It was bordered in front by a long, wide drive, like a square, sheltered from the street by a low ivy-covered wall and the branches of the oak trees. At the back was an acre of land, wild and sprawling, that sloped down to the boundary of a wash, a barren concrete aqueduct eight or ten feet across, carrying the water from the streams in the hills. The yard there was covered for the most part by trees of all kinds—huge dark oaks that had given the place its name; plum trees on the slope of the hill that would bloom in spring into an ocean of white blossoms; towering elm and willow and sycamore whose branches made a tangle in the sky at the base of the hill; at the very back border a cluster of fruit trees: fig, orange, lemon, grapefruit, and walnut, in a kind of forgotten arbor; and one huge, solitary palm with the mountains behind it. After I had left home, when I would think at first of going back, I thought of the trees, and I could imagine only happiness there.

Under the trees were gardens that she had planted with her own hands when she was still young, the four of us milling about around her: white Easter lilies, iris, tulips, and tiny white cockleshells beneath the plum trees on the slope; a curved wall of daffodil and wild rose beneath a grove of sycamore; and near the lawn at the top of the hill a terrace of roses and birds-of-paradise. At the front of the house, under the breakfast room windows, were azalea, roses, lilies, camellia, and one dark shining banana tree, and under my bedroom windows, gardenia.

At nighttime, if the moon was new or not very bright, you could stand at the glass doors in the room lined with bookshelves and look down into the yard beneath the trees, and it was as though you were staring into a great black pool that gave back no reflection at all so that you would only feel yourself drawn farther and farther down, searching its depth for something reflecting light there. But there would be none.

If you were to walk down there on such a night, with the branches above you, no light would reach you from the house above, and you would find yourself in complete darkness. Then everything around you would seem to move in very close, and every sound become bright and sharp, because there was nothing anymore to see. This was how I learned to no longer be afraid in the dark, how darkness first became a friend.

On the west side of the property a long brick stairway led down from the top where the house stood, in terraces, to the bottom of the hill where the yard leveled off. Once, coming home to visit, I left the house and made my way to that side where the steps start, near a terrace of roses and a small lemon tree. I walked to the bottom and sat down on the last step. The trees on the north side of the yard, the sycamore and elm, were moving in the wind. I closed my eyes: silver and green wind poured down through the leaves like the rush of waves on a beach, grays and browns and gold of sun through leaves, wave after wave like a dance, the trembling and bowing of the trunks and their limbs rocking me, dizzyingly, turning round and round in their song like a child on a sand wheel. It struck me: that sound they made had been part of my memory from the earliest times, a sound like none other I have ever known, one I would find only in that place.

I wished then that I could have remembered it all, through everything that had happened. I wished that I could have always known that no matter what happened, those trees, the wind, the mountains towering blue and hard against the sky, would still be there, standing quietly since the beginning as they did now and that I would come back to them. The trees would still be holding themselves against the sky, and the wind would not have died. These things were not like people; they were constant, unchanging. I missed them then, sitting there on the steps. I missed that place for the time I had been gone and for when I would leave again. Because it had endured. And I had seen so little that had endured in such a graceful way.

I sat frozen and quiet, listening to something that seemed far away, something familiar rising through the layers of wind like reflections shining from the bottom of a pool. Another of the little girl-child ghosts, a much younger me looking up through the layers of time at who I had become, sitting on the last of the brick steps in the sun.

They say it's the survival of something too painful, something unthinkable, that makes that break occur: the perfect discreet and hidden change that separates us from the witness, the part of ourselves who knows everything we have seen or lived through. And we no longer recognize or remember certain experiences, but we'll do things we cannot recall. Only the people around us notice the effect of the other side—the break with reality they call psychosis.

As children we never endured anything like that, not like she had. Nothing so impossible to remember that we had to pretend, even to ourselves. Instead, we just let the worst of our memories float away. Then we'd come back to that place and feel as though we were being followed by someone or something that had been waiting for us, never quite alone even there, in what had been one of the loneliest of places.

14

Hurting Her

Arcadia 1962

They're hurting her.

I'm not sure what happened . . . she was trying to leave, she just wanted to go out, but they wouldn't let her go. They didn't want her to go. She was okay—that's what I remember. Sometimes she wouldn't be, but this wasn't one of those times. She'd done her hair, which was pinned up still; she'd covered it with a scarf to wear while she waited for it to set. Then she would brush it out.

They stopped her at the front door; she had her purse. She was crying and I was crying, standing in a little alcove where the hallways met, my cousin holding me, trying to hush me. But we were just standing there, watching. There was screaming. My screaming? Their screaming? My aunts were pulling on her, trying to pull her away from the door, and she was crying. They were hurting her.

15

The Young Girl

Arcadia 1989

Later, in her room, at the top of her closet I found something—a scrapbook she had made when she was young, with a black cover and something embossed at the corner. I knelt on the floor of the closet to see what she had collected there in the books from her childhood, a part of her as young and hopeful as any I had ever known in myself. She was even more naive and delicate than I had been. The scrapbook held letters she had been sent, cards filled with affectionate expressions, pictures she had clipped from magazines: a beautiful dress, curtains for a house, postcards from places not very far from home. To see all of this, in the light of the end of her life, made a silent and painful awakening—the remnants of things she'd dreamt about, in bits and pieces on those pages. Now I could match the things I had seen all my life in some ragged caricature to these secret, hidden moments where they had begun. I grieved for her and felt that sinking in my body at the sudden awareness that the young girl had been there all the time without ever being seen. I was stunned.

She had seen a different kind of darkness than the one she would show me, her child. In watching her I could see only the effect it had had, the way a shadow changes the color of something. And that *something* was different still from what she had actually known, an effect after time—not the first moment, when her eyes had met the things that made her turn inward.

I remembered a summer night:

I'd been brought into the family room with my brothers and sister and was told to stay there. But the doorbell rings and I push the sliding door open and wander into the entry hall. I am barely four years old. There are men in spotless white clothing who say things I cannot hear . . . but it is not for my mother that they have come on this night of unusual stillness, these men with their perfect white clothing, their strangely calm voices. It is not my mother but the body of the young girl that they have lifted from her bed and lain on the little cot with wheels to bring down the hallway toward the door, while I wait in confusion, watching their invasion motionlessly from my hidden place by the stone wall. It is not my mother but the young girl whom they carry in this way, pale and lifeless but still alive, through the door of our house and out into the warmth and flower scent of the summer night.

She isn't thinking anymore about the beautiful dress or the brocade pillow—something to sew—or the garden she plans to make while her children are playing, the children she'll one day have. She's not thinking of any of that now. She's not thinking about the pink stationary with the little dog in the corner, inscribed with her name, or the songs she sings, or how she'll do her hair, how lovely she'll look . . . She had been there all along, even let me see her, and I had known her instinctively, *as every child knows the innocence of her mother.*

I felt again, those many years later, how badly I had wanted to protect her against that darkness which I would never find words to describe. How I had failed, powerless and overwhelmed by love, while she made her descent. I remembered now: it was not my mother whom I had seen standing at the mirror before her dressing table, crying, while she tore at her face and hair with her own hands. Not my mother in whose eyes I first saw the explosion of something that was more than terror, something beyond the surrender that had haunted her expression. It had been the face of a young girl, the eyes of a young girl suddenly remembering what had happened to her, as if she were looking back on the years of her life as they drifted by, a swimmer suddenly realizing she has drifted hopelessly far from shore, knowing she will never get back now, that she'll die in the water.

Now I had become the woman of dark beauty in the photograph of the bougainvillea, seated with her own dark-eyed firstborn girl-child in her arms just a few weeks old. I had become the young woman whose eyes glowed with the heat of joy, in love with her first child, a grace surrounding us as palpable as the electric aura of desire. A year from then my own daughter would be seated in the same spot under the sycamore tree where I had once been placed for a photograph, in my tiny pink dress and pearl buttons, thirty years before. She would hear the wind above her, like waves in an ocean in the sky, rushing down through the canopy of the trees, as I had heard it in my memory all my life. How could I make it come out differently for us?

16

Arcadia

1963

I wake in the night and try to go to her. Sliding down the side of my bed to touch the floor, I pad down the short, dark hallway that leads to their room. The hardwood floors creak, a dry cracking sound in the darkness. I stand in the doorway for a moment. The ever-present night-light from my parents' bathroom illuminates the statues on their dresser, the statues I have stared at lying awake between my parents sometimes in their bed at night—Mary in her long blue mantle, St. Joseph in red, on either side of a tall jewelry case.

No one is lying on her side of the bed. I call out to her, then ask, "Where is Mommy?"

My father is awake, or I have woken him.

"She's gone away for a little while," he tells me.

I can't think of anything to say. I know he doesn't like for me to come into their bed at night. I don't remember anything that's happened. I miss her terribly. I turn around and go back down the hall to my room.

17

Dusk

1971

She loved to walk on summer nights. The neighborhood was so
lovely, and it was always cooler outside in the dusk than inside
the house at that time of day. She wanted him to walk with her, but
he wouldn't. I don't know what it meant to him, whether he was
tired from the long day of work or just did not want to converse.
She wanted him to walk with her the way the other couples did,
but when he wouldn't she would sometimes take me. I would hold
her hand and we would make our way up toward the northwest
part of the block first.

One night we stopped in at her friend's house, a woman who
had a daughter Mara's age. The house was white, two stories, a Cape
Cod–style bungalow with a small balcony on the second story
above the front door. The woman who lived there had been left by
her husband. He was a hunter, for sport. He'd been in Alaska and
had somehow been cornered by his quarry, had tried to escape by
climbing a tree but was followed by the bear that went up after him
and ripped his shoulder out. While they spoke about him, I could

hear his wife's longing. All these things had happened to him, she'd nursed him back to health, but here she was, alone now. And he was off somewhere, up another tree. I understood this somehow, as young as I was.

We sat in her living room, my mother and she sipping their drinks and talking. I loved being in an unfamiliar house, perfectly kept, like the pictures of homes in my mother's magazines, and smelling of new smells, all pleasant and interesting: the furniture polish, the carpets, the wax on the floors.

Another time she came to the door but didn't want us to come in. I was embarrassed for my mother, that we would be turned away. But she had been drinking, the woman who was our friend.

18

The Nightmare
Before Christmas

Arcadia 1992

That autumn, Steven, Jenny, and I go down to empty the house.
Ian meets us there. My father had been brought away months
before, too old and frail to live alone anymore. I want one last
autumn holiday in this house before it's gone.

One evening after dark, we go out—Ian, Jenny, and I—to the
theater. Brush fires have broken out up and down the state, pushed
in the south into a frenzy by the hot and powerful Santa Ana winds
from the northeast. As we walk out to the car, the fires are still
smoldering in the hills to the east, tiny flares of orange and black
dotting the walls of the canyons.

Sitting in the dark of the theater we are regaled with images
of tiny stick figures wandering through a landscape of eternal darkness. We watch these figures tumbling through space, the lights
from the screen flickering against our upturned faces as their
narrow forms hold tenaciously to life, the principalities of darkness

waging war against their fragile grasp. These surreal creatures are averting disaster through impossibly narrow escape. There is love amid all this chaos, and good triumphs. The picture is *The Nightmare Before Christmas*.

Emerging into our own smoke-covered night, Jenny is bewildered but safe in my arms. We scan the hills where the fires are sparkling, the billows of ash making even darker shadows against the sky. Halloween is coming. Tomorrow we will prepare.

Halloween

Jenny has chosen a tiny white lace bride's dress as her costume for this night, not so different from the bride last night. With her hair drawn up on top of her head and little tendrils falling, tiny lips rouged, she poses on the cool white stone outside the front door in the light of the jack-o-lanterns. My brother Kyle and his wife kneel beside her for a snapshot. There is a new peacefulness in the house, and I can think only of how much I loved growing up there—not for what we went through, but for its shelter and the beauty and magic that was everywhere. We take flashlights and coats and venture into a mild Indian summer night, making our last pilgrimage through the wide, dark streets that were the place of my own childhood fantasies on thirteen separate Halloween nights, for thirteen years before I went away.

Each house we pass holds memories. Almost all the people I once knew are gone now, but their spirits are still with me as though it were just yesterday when I saw them last. As we walk, the night becomes a masquerade that is peopled less with living, breathing revelers than with these sweet and wild spirits in costumes of the lives they once knew, spirits who have long since crossed to a place I will not find by growing up. Tonight, they return and fly through my waking dream like shadows of birds startled in a rush against the sun.

At the end of the drive, we cross to the first house across the way, where the lady with the orange dress lived, in her Cinderella house that reminded me always of pumpkins and candles and warm autumn evenings, and my mother's wool suit of burnt umber and orange. Even now, the front lawns are deep and lush, and peacock chicks wander between the bushes, waiting for magical transformation.

We make our way west up a long street to a shaded bungalow, white and pale green, where I'd spend summer mornings feeding the cats for Mrs. Decker, who traveled alone since her husband had died. She was tiny, old, and perfect; her dresses and hair so carefully done. She'd welcome us, me and my other little friends from the neighborhood, into the cool darkness of her house, showing us what to do in her absence. Her gentle kindness and the perfect order of her house encircle me again, the rooms waiting in the shadow beneath the oaks, rooms I often had not wanted to leave for the peacefulness she kept there. Even now, in adulthood, her house appears in my dreams, a place I long for but do not hope to find.

At the top of the long winding block, where we turn to go north, is the house where Jeanette lived. She was a year older than me, with blonde hair that hung in thick ropes down her back, and a terrifyingly wild dog that her parents kept chained at the back of their yard. Despite our closeness in age, Jeanette represented a foreign world to me, a world that frightened me: of boys at the public school, and freedom to run wild at night, and a necessity of being tougher than I knew how to be, in ways different from the only ones I knew. And yet, knowing she moved in that world, so young, just like me, made me feel afraid for her sake. Oddly, I would never have chosen to trade places with her, although my own world became at least as hard to survive.

We walk north one short block to the streets on the other side, then west a quarter mile in the shadow of the mountains, the canyons, the boundary of anything I had known: what had been "the rest of the world" to me then.

There is a mysterious house there, one I had never seen anyone enter or leave, standing just as before—two stories, white and shadowed in the broad canopy of oak leaves from the hundred-year-old trees in front. I search for signs of change and find them. Someone has built a support for the failing tree and trimmed away branches. A new family has come to live there.

We continue down the hills, past the brick pillars and white rail fences of the Sidden's mansion: I think of another day, long ago, my tiny hand being held by someone—my mother?—walking along with her and her friend, when I'd heard the whispered conversation of the women: "She's dying . . . and so young . . . all of those children he'll be left to raise alone . . ." I don't know when that was, how old I'd been, but they used to take me swimming, the daughters who lived in that house. I remember lying in the shuttered dark of the bedroom I'd shared with Mara as a child, napping there alone, barely two years old, when I heard their voices outside on the drive, then at the front door, and my mother's steps down the long, dark hallway. I'd pretended to be asleep, hiding beneath the covers at the foot of the bed, but was finally carried amid the clamor of their young voices, their delight and affection, and set down in the bathroom to be dressed in one of the little suits my cousins had once worn, a seersucker jumpsuit still smelling of pool smells, chlorine, and Coppertone—smells I would learn to love. These girls would take me with them that afternoon, and I would learn to swim in the deepest part of the pool before that summer ended, amazing the adults and older children, and I would love water for the rest of my life. But I would never remember their faces, or any other part of that day, or any other thing about their lives, only that whispered conversation outside the gates where they lived and the half know-ing a mystery of fear at the middle of their world.

At the end of a little hill, where we would normally turn south to walk home, we walk farther ahead around another curve that leads to Jimmy's old house: a Southern colonial with tall white pillars in front supporting a second story shaded by another of the ancient oak trees, the lawn under that shade darker and more lush than anywhere else. Jimmy was my age, in my class at school, tall and serious and sweet, with not much to say and little else that I remember but this one thing: he had a little sister different from all the other children, mentally disabled somehow in a way that we were too young to understand, who somehow wore an endearing but perpetually puzzled expression. There was something about Jimmy that I learned one day, playing on a rare occasion near his house with my friends: I saw him outside with his sister, his hand on her shoulder, the sweetness of his voice, his leaning down to look into her eyes, the way he said her name, a little plaintively, and his questions to her, trying to keep her from doing something that would have put her in harm's way.

It was one of the first times I began to realize the difference between the image I might form of someone and who they might really be, or to think about the difference between the facade I presented at school and the experiences I had had privately, the things that were not talked about, not allowable in any ordinary conversation, or even one imagined.

Now, above us, the webs of oak leaves were pouring their shadows onto the grass in the fading light, the hundreds of leaves with tiny pointed edges like the corners of shapes in a spiderweb, edges that cut our fingers when we were young, until we learned not to gather them with our bare hands, leaves that were stiff and strong and made good boats for floating with tiny seed people down the rivulets of rain at the edges of the curb, but not for gathering to lie in. The sound of Jimmy's voice on the lawn, calling to his sister, and the vision of them standing together beneath the huge dark limbs of the tree waver and fall into the moist darkness of the grass beneath that tree, into the green pool the leaves and light have made, sinking toward a place we cannot see, a perfect burial.

I cannot know what became of them, but I want to wonder, will always want to wonder, to keep alive the memory of him as I knew him then—tall for his age and quiet, unknowingly carrying that weight of love.

Just across from Jimmy's house, on the same block at the very end, was the house that once belonged to one of my father's colleagues. The low white bungalow with rose gardens beneath the windows and a lawn in front was not sheltered like the other houses, everything set out squarely for anyone to see, but the windows had always been covered, the shades and shutters closed. As children we had imagined she was standing in the darkness behind one of them, watching us as we walked or rode by. There had been a horrible accident, the whole family together in the car, but it was their daughter who'd been the most severely injured, left brain dead. Her mother could not recover; people said she'd lost her mind, and we imagined her there, knowing she had stopped coming out. The father left and remarried.

I remember my mother taking me with her one day to see the woman who had once been her friend. She tried to bring her something, the two of us standing at the front door, but no one would answer. Never before had I known anyone who would not trust my mother. I remember the disappointment in her face at being unable to help her friend, who remained behind those doors and never emerged again. Sometimes we would see her son's bright red sports car parked in the driveway at night or on a weekend morning, when he would bring her things. What I could not have understood then, what I would wonder at tentatively years later, as though vaguely aware of a shadow at the edge of my vision which I had never turned to face, was this: what it must have been like for my mother, seeing her friend give up a struggle she herself continued to fight with only the most tentative of hopes.

Somehow that morning, the morning my mother tried to visit, is linked in my memory with another day: We're standing in the drive by the old station wagon, at our house, and I've accidentally caught my finger in the car door closing. I remember as though it were yesterday, looking down through the burning pain and seeing, for the first time in my young life, a part of my own body suddenly unrecognizable: pale, white, and bloodless, the thickness of skin oddly bunched up in a wound, everything torn and mangled against the bone. My mother took me then to the only doctor she knew close by, and it was not my father, who worked downtown. It was the husband of her friend, the woman in the bungalow, working at a clinic near our house.

"It's a compound fracture," my mother would say later, describing it to friends and to my father, who, on this one occasion, had not been the one to set the bone and stitch the broken skin, though he would have taken everything off to look at the work.

This would be what I would always remember of that family: the rose garden and the perfect white-shingled bungalow that their father had abandoned, the story of their accident in the car, and seeing him for the first time the morning I'd crushed my finger and thinking, *That's your house; you've left them* and not wanting him to touch me. Because my own father told us the opposite all the time, at every opportunity away from the house and my mother, which was only on Sunday mornings when my youngest brother and I were very young, and usually after she had tried to hurt us or herself. In the dirty streets of downtown Los Angeles, where he'd brought us with him to work and chapel, he would rest one of his hands on each of our shoulders as we walked on either side of him.

"Always remember," he'd say, "I'll never leave you. *Never.* Always remember that."

It was only later that I would learn: his own mother had taken her five surviving children and left his father, finding somewhere else to raise them alone in the poor neighborhoods of New York City when he was still a young boy.

We turn back, heading west toward home. We come back to the curve where we'd started, only from the other side, past the Mortons' mansion, the wide lawns, to that curve near our driveway or just before, by the hedges. The place where the dog had died. And I remember again: a summer's day and Jeanette's mother.

She'd been racing home that afternoon in a bright orange sports car when we heard the screech of brakes and a sudden ominous silence. They came for my father. I was eight. Because it was summertime, he was taking his short vacation or they would not have found him there. He went into the street in one of the perfect dark suits he wore and knelt under the car to lift the body of the neighbor's beautiful Afghan dog that was trapped under the wheels. Jeanette's mother said the dog had darted out from the hedge and been dragged under the wheels before she could stop.

My father was rarely ever seen in our neighborhood, except arriving and departing, and I could feel the reverence everyone felt for him in that moment. The neighbor children and I huddled in a little circle around them, watching my father wrap the dog in a blanket, a huge pool of blood spreading out around his knees. The older girls who lived next door were crying and asked if he could do anything to save their dog's life. Only I seemed to realize then that my father had seldom, if ever, let himself touch our animals, though he was often solicitous for their well-being and meals. I remember feeling helplessly proud of him, bewildered by the tenderness he now displayed. He offered to take the animal in, which he did, but told us that it had gone into shock and would not survive.

19

Arcadia

July 1985

My body is her body. I see that now, though before when she was alive, I could not. I was young and she had been ravaged by illness and addiction.

We'd stood in my bathroom, in the house where I'd grown up, with the long bank of mirrors, reflections on three sides, and she had taken out the dresses she'd worn in her youth and the early part of her marriage. I was twenty-four. Each one fit me like a glove, all of them as though they had been fitted especially to me, following each line and curve of my own body as if they had been sewn onto me.

My body was her body, half an inch shorter and perhaps a little larger boned, I can't say for sure. My sister reminded me later: she would have worn corsets and girdles with the dresses, and I slipped them on with nothing, but I was thinner then.

She looked up into the mirror and regarded my reflection. In my memory she looks young and beautiful too, as she had in her forties, dark softness of hair curved around her face, limpid eyes, tall. But I know that's not what she looked like then. She was two years shy of her death.

She looked at me in the mirror and said, "We'll make a model of you yet,"—an odd, incongruous remark.

20

Spirits

Arcadia 1992

On the last morning that we were there, the house was empty. We had spent the past several days in the strange process of closure: excavating the remnants of my parents' lives from closets, cupboards, attic, and safe spaces. Through all this the house seemed passive, only a shell of her former self, furnished with whatever we could not dispose of, things at once irreplaceable and useless, rescued by our indecision.

I imagined her before our arrival, standing empty in those intervening months after my father was gone. I knew what it was like to be there alone; I imagined her walls in the peaceful stillness of the afternoon, the change of coolness at night, the soundlessness, and then the suddenness of our arrival, receiving our voices and footsteps, all the spirits quieting while she waited in submission.

Jenny followed me as I worked, sometimes settling nearby to play with one thing or another, talking to herself in the sweet, guileless way a toddler talks, fascinated by the many things her grandparents had collected and the novelty of exploring them. I sometimes paused to watch her. In her imagination she transformed each object she found into whatever she needed for her stories, things completely "other than what they were." The collection of tiny porcelain birds my mother had given me became creatures from books we had read together, Jenny and I. Little wooden dolls spoke of things they had never before imagined, waiting on their shelves in the library—events from my daughter's and my times together, nothing the dolls had seen. In her tiny hands, they all had new lives.

The more we removed, the more crowded the house became. She filled with the ghosts of young girls: daughters, sisters, aunts, all the women whose lives I'd dreamt about, women my mother had spoken of, women who had cared for me, whose secrets I had wondered at, all returned in the phantom forms of childhood, the gentle bodies in which they'd lived when their hopefulness and dreams were alive.

They spilled into the rooms from those opened places, disturbed with the dust, tumbling down from the shelves and the boxes with remnants of the cool and bustling mornings, when the scent of roses and gardenia were heavy in the air, mixed with the soft, dusty smell of summer coming through the windows left open in the night. They pushed out from behind heavy curtains in forgotten corners of the rooms, through melancholy afternoons when the rain could be heard falling softly through the leaves of the oak trees, tapping gently on the roof at first until gathering weight and blanketing the world.

We could not persuade them to rest again. We could not put any of it back; we could not take any of it with us, this stuff of memory to which they were attached. At night when we were sleeping, they gathered above our beds, above our gently breathing bodies, rising above the lace canopies, through ceilings, attic, and roof to the rain of ash coming down from the hills. The ashes falling softly against them made a mantle that gave their flight form, a paler gray cloud against the smoky gray black of the sky. When they got to the hills, they stepped into the towers of smoke above the fire and were carried on these to the stars, never to be seen again. I had no choice but to watch them go.

I don't need to pretend it was magical, how Jenny came to understand. We were in their bedroom, my parents' room, which was empty, finally. I looked at the space where the bed had been, where my mother had slept and not slept, where I had lain with her to comfort her. I could remember doing this even as a child. I looked at the paper she had chosen for the walls: silver with pale lavender fleur-de-lis. The ivory curtains with lavender ties. There had been a lavender carpet, a gold bedspread. She had chosen each one of those accessories so carefully. I had been about five or six years old.

Suddenly I did not know how to leave. I couldn't imagine *never* being able to come back. In the stillness of her room, I felt her there again, watching us. Watching me but unable to speak.

"Goodbye," I said out loud.

My voice was hollow against the bare wood of the floors and the huge glass panes looking out onto the garden, the roses she had planted, the plum trees that would bloom again into an ocean of pink and white on the hill, and in her rock garden the startling oranges of the birds-of-paradise. Was it only my voice that made her real?

"Goodbye, Mom."

Following behind me, as I walked back to the door, Jenny's small voice asked, puzzled, "Who are you talking to? Who's here?"

I turned to her, embarrassed not so much by what I'd said (which are the only words I had spoken to my mother, silently or aloud, since her dying) as by the fact that I'd forgotten Jenny would hear me. She stared up at me then, wide-eyed and patient, awaiting a simple explanation that would help everything make sense, this whole new person, my daughter, in the place where I was young.

I looked at her. I felt my mother waiting. When we were gone, her spirit would follow to the smoke in the hills.

"Your grandmother loved this house," I told her gently. "I'm just saying goodbye."

21

Montana

August 1972

There was another bridge once. It was summertime; I was twelve. We had taken a bus—my mother, her sister Elke, and I—across the broad fields of Montana grassland. It was prairie like the Kansas of *The Wizard of Oz* I had thought, continuing on endlessly with nothing to see in either direction. We came to the little mining town, almost deserted now, everything quiet; night was falling. The bus left us near a tavern. We walked up a hill past the slack pile—the waste from the strip mining in a mountain of black—to the little cabin I had seen for the first time several years before, when my grandfather was still alive and I was just three. But nine years had passed since that summer.

At the top of the hill the sun was leaving a glare of reddish gold on the mountains to the east. Inside the little wooden gate, the cabin stood, the white paint of the clapboards and a single small, curtained window on the side set closest to the road. A pump for water stood on one side of the walkway just outside the door, as well as some outhouses at the far end of the little yard, made from long planks that had darkened and splintered in the sun and winter snow. My mother had been *born* here.

In the morning Elke made us something to eat on the little wood-burning stove, and we washed from a basin and dressed in the darkness together, the curtains of the room still drawn against the morning heat. Then we walked back down the hill into the town.

Strolling through the town past the old buildings, Elke pointed to one with walls of brick that would have left most of the sidewalk in shadow except for the position of the sun high overhead. It was their old high school, she told me, and I remembered the stories I'd been told of my mother taking her music lessons there from the nuns. She had been a great favorite of theirs, her sisters had said.

We left the main street and took a pathway that wound through a grove of trees and dusty grass fields. That was when we found the bridge. We came upon it in a sudden way, standing together on the banks of the river, on the outskirts of the town. I don't remember anything about where I had thought we were going. I only remember those few moments of perfect stillness when the leaves of trees growing close and massed finally broke, and we were standing beside the rock bed cut in the dry earth, now choked with the tall grasses and weeds. I asked my mother a question and she answered me as we stood with the bridge hanging before us.

The sight of it was a surprise after everything else I had seen in the town: ropes laced up from the bank at our feet to form the span, the suggestion of sides, and a handrail; but the vines had grown so thickly, tangled and choked across her, it was impossible to tell where they might have broken the bindings. Her floor was an invitation that was tantalizing and impossible all at once.

From where I stood on the bank, she looked ancient and unreal, the play of dusty July light that filtered through the trees, making her glow softly. All the time I was there, everything else about the town had seemed vacant to me, a despair I felt but could not name or find a beginning to, mirrored perfectly in the broken roads and the buildings whose shadows fell over us. But the bridge was different, hanging delicately over her memory of the stream, ravaged once by her setting and now forgotten. Yet what had been left behind remains set apart in memory from everything else about that summer. On the bridge I could see, magically, the light of the past, of another time, of different leaves falling, different shadows, the sounds of animals rustling in the grass beneath the light of a different moon at night and the warmth of a different sun, when everything that lay beneath that sky was still new and young. My mother had asked me to go back with her. She was afraid to go there alone.

The summer that I saw the bridge glowing softly in the July sun was the same summer that my mother took me with her to see Naomi. They had grown up together, and Naomi was still there in the town.

We had taken a ride from a man in a dusty blue truck, past the outskirts of the town to where a long dirt track came out to meet the highway. We'd walked down toward a little yellow house that stood close to the track at the edge of a field of dark turned earth, near a cluster of trees.

Inside the house I remember feeling suddenly bewildered, as though I had stepped into a place that made me afraid of being left behind, a place I might soon want to leave. We sat down at a table in the kitchen near a long window that looked out over the field. It was hot, we were all a little wilted, and flies wove lazily above us, floating at levels in the air above the table like tiny planes in loose formation, an escort for a mission of espionage, pretending to other things. The women sat below these, their fingers resting gently laced against the sides of cool cans of beer.

Every now and then Naomi would get up and stand with her back against the edge of the counter, holding her cigarette, surveying us. She was striking: part Cherokee and Slavic mixed, with dark hair and dark eyes like my mother's, tall and lanky like my mother also; but I remember the two of them seeming beautiful in opposite ways. Naomi wore bright red lipstick, and her fingernails were painted the same shade, and so were her toes, in their rubber sandals. Glancing at me, she would pretend to wonder where her young daughters had disappeared to. They were "around somewhere," she said, and should be back any minute.

I knew something about my mother's friend, but I don't remember how I knew or when it was supposed to have happened, perhaps the night before our visit. It had stayed in my mind like something incomprehensible, something to try to understand later by myself: there had been drinking, an argument, and her boyfriend, or the man she lived with, had dragged her outside and locked her out of the house in the dark without any clothes on. She'd had to go for help like that.

That afternoon, standing in Naomi's kitchen listening to the women talk, I understood only that Naomi was not like my mother. My mother was happy at certain times and desperately unhappy at other times and seemed always to be waiting patiently, in between the two, to see what kind of time it was going to be. On the day that I had first seen her, Naomi seemed already to know what kind of time she was going to be having for the rest of her life, and to have decided to practice not caring. I knew that my mother overlooked and forgave this difference in her friend by the careful quiet blankness I felt in her when we were there together, as though she were making herself still on purpose, not to show something she was feeling. And I knew Naomi could tell and was pretending that she hadn't noticed and that together they were silently forgiving each other for it having to be that way, or for something only they understood.

Later that next winter when I was older, sitting at the dinner table in my uncle Evan's farmhouse, he would touch on that thing about Naomi that I had not been able to name. Something had happened to her again. He'd heard about it in town, something that seemed to have happened to her many times before, and he unburdened himself of the story in broken sentences, speaking more to my aunt than to his daughters or to me. Though I never understood exactly what it was, I knew it had something to do with a man and Naomi being hurt, like the night before I'd met her. I could see my uncle Evan holding a hidden picture in his mind, thinking of her, the weight of which made him appear suddenly very tired, his expression taking on a weariness and disbelief, which in our innocence we returned with silence. He told us not to judge her, that her heart was good.

Part IV

22

San Francisco Bay Area

1989

My mother was the first to die. In the twenty-four months' time which began that fall just before Jenny's birth, she was the first of her family, the first of the adult children to die.

At the same time, her brother Evan lay fighting a different kind of cancer. One of my aunts called me from Helena. Evan kept remembering something about when they were young, how my mother had wanted to hold his hand as they walked to school for his first day, and how sweet she'd been despite his refusal to submit to her.

Then I remembered something about that winter so many years before, when I was fourteen, the winter I had come to live with his family, something my uncle had only admitted privately to my cousin Elaine, who repeated it later to me: how it pained her father to look up and see me sitting across from him at the table in the farmhouse with his own daughters, that it was like looking up and seeing my mother there at the same age. We looked so much alike, time turning backward thirty years, and the eeriness of it.

A small collection of photographs arrived in the mail a few weeks later, from Elke: tiny sepia prints. One showed Evan and my mother, the two youngest, sitting next to one another on a walkway at the mining camp, near the gate in front of the little cabin where they grew up. They were both thin. Evan is sitting in the dust with his knees pulled up under his chin, all of eleven years old, beaming a proud smile, and Marni, my mother, is next to him, her hair curled and pinned neatly for the occasion, only there is a cloth beneath her protecting her skirt from the dirt that surrounds them.

In another print, my mother is wearing a flowered dress and riding a bicycle in a wide, empty street that's deeply rutted, with a tiny cabin in the background behind her and a metal shack beside it, a small fence guarding these from the road. She has turned the handlebars toward the camera while balancing on the pedals, her dark hair making a cloud around her face.

The other pictures were familiar to me. The one of her First Communion: she is dressed in white from head to toe with a veil that falls to the edge of her dress, just above her knees, which are large and strong for her small frame, her long legs covered in white stockings. Her hands are clasped together holding something that disappears against the white of her dress, a missal with its tiny gold-embossed cross. In this picture, as in another formal portrait taken several years later, her eyes are the same inscrutable dark pools that look somewhere beyond the viewer, her gaze refusing to be met.

After my mother, her brother Evan was the next to die, exactly one year later. Jenny was just beginning to walk, and the season had come again with the scent of wood smoke in the cold air and the leaves turning. I thought: "It's gone now, taken from out of the world"—his spark, the momentum of his sheer physical strength, a presence so different from anything I had ever known.

The pictures of him in his youth had surprised me. He'd looked tall and thin then, even gangly. But years of work on his farm and in his ironworks shop in the town had filled him out, adding bulk to his arms and chest so that he seemed massive to me when I was growing up, broad-shouldered and wide, with a stride that was long for his height. His head was shiny and nearly hairless, like Popeye's. Only his features hinted at the boy he had left behind in the photographs: a wide mouth, so ready to smile, his sharply pointed nose, dark sparkling eyes. He would come home in the afternoons for lunch in the summer when I was visiting, wearing his green work shirt and trousers, and smelling of sweat and oil and smoke from the shop. He would sweep us off our feet when we met him at the porch in the years when we were still old enough to be picked up, our legs dangling over his arms, the screen door slamming, his affection breaking against us like an unexpected wave, lifting us into the air. His girls were used to that, but I would hold myself still in his arms, as always, wondering what was going to happen. And always the wave that he'd become would sweep past me, setting me back down again on its way, gently.

My aunt Nina would have prepared a huge meal, and we would all sit down together for lunch, and then he would drive back into town and return again in the evening. Perhaps I waited for his coming home, as I had learned to wait for that of my father's, at the end of the day: a time when everyone would sit down together, adults and children alike, and focus on something important, which was whatever he had to say. The difference perhaps was that Evan offered me more attention at the table in those few summers than my father was able to give me until the very last years of his life.

Evan took with him out of the world that energy which, out of some graceful mercy for himself and us, had channeled itself into a sense of humor that was larger than life, so surprisingly honest it held everyone in a rapt attention bordering on awe, broken only by the laughter he could play from us.

Evan had come to live with our family in California after the Korean War for a few months, "to rest," they'd told me when I was young. But later I learned he needed help from my father's colleagues. "Shellshock" they called it. There is an old Native

American saying about one who "swallows the snake" to keep its power. I thought of this after Evan died.

We would go back with him that time—my mother, my sister and brothers and I—ahead of my father, Evan driving us across the long expanse of desert outside Los Angeles, across the western states and into the Rocky Mountains to reach his home. My father would come later in the summer to meet us and bring us back home.

The two men were as different from one another as could be imagined, and even as a child I realized that my uncle was being patient. We were on his turf, and he could afford to be. My father loved the chance to be taken out fishing, to see the country, to hear the stories of the hunting season. They had both been born into poverty, but whatever he might have lived through in his youth, the rest of my father's life had placed him in a world as far from the one my uncle occupied as possible. While Evan was boisterous, passionate, and funny, my father was reserved, silent most of the time and taciturn, and I had learned to expect from him only a polite facade of amusement in company, and in private only detachment or anger.

Later, when I would come to live with Evan and Nina that brief December, the extent of Evan's patience would be made clear to me, how he thought something should have been done earlier for my mother, the anger that he'd had to hold in for years. And Elaine would tell me: my father thought *your* father left her "flapping in the wind."

But in those earlier days none of this was clear to me in any conscious way, except the faintest feeling of something missing between my father and myself, like a pale shadow as only a child would feel it, without words and even without knowing, just by virtue of the time spent watching my uncle with his own girls.

He'd had three, each a few years apart. They said Alexis was his boy, and she learned to keep up with him, the two of them hunting and fishing together, driving the tractors, and working the little ranch. But she grew up to be beautiful, voluptuous, and sensitive, fortified by his masculinity and her mother's quiet strength. She and Mara were a year apart, Elaine a year younger than they, and Shari a year younger than I.

After working in the house and garden in the mornings, some afternoons we were idle and restless. One evening near dusk we wandered into a thicket. The adults were inside the house; we'd had dinner and were playing badminton on the tiny lawn when someone mentioned the wasps' nest. We wanted to see! The five of us children crowded into the tiny opening in the trees, a cavern of pale green leaves at the edge of the field. We climbed in together, pushing the branches aside, one after another. And then, in the sudden quiet, Kyle pulled up his racket and swung. A gray cloud poured from the nest, which had exploded in a mass of mud and twigs, crumbling like a broken gourd pouring its seeds on the ground.

Everyone was pushing to get out and away. Alexis and I had gone in first and were trapped at the back; at least I was, and she stayed with me and told me to hold very still. Together we watched the mass of wasps swarm, flying out through the opening behind everyone else, except for one that settled purposefully on my forearm and slowly burrowed in, its tiny insect dance becoming suddenly still. It made a tingling and burning unlike anything I had felt before, and no way to stop it. We emerged, my face stained with tears, and made our way up to the house after the others. The adults had been relaxing in their usual ritual of after-dinner drinks and conversation. I have the vaguest memory of my father listening to the story calmly, as if this once, in front of everyone, he could not feign indifference; he appeared sincerely sorry for this most recent consequence of my brother's inexplicably wild behavior, and weariedly asked Kyle what the point was, after all, in doing something like that? It was a rhetorical question. I don't remember my aunt and uncle saying anything just then, except for Alexis to take me out and make a poultice of mud to take the sting away.

Sixteen years later, in the fall, one year after my mother was gone, Evan lay on his own deathbed, sardonic to the end. My aunts would call and tell me the things he said, how he still brought them up short with his humor. When they complained about anything too much, he would remind them gently that, in fact, it was *he* who was dying.

Then twelve months later it was my grandmother, in her sleep. And then finally, Aunt Lara, suddenly, in Baltimore. It was as though someone had come to collect them all for a meeting scheduled in that special season, on the other side, leaving the other three sisters behind, the ones who had never wandered far from home.

But Evan remembered something else before he died. Strangely, as if breaking a spell, the key to Pandora's box, at the edge of his own end, he brought forth this story, one I'd been waiting to discover for the greater part of my life, seeking some connection to something real.

They'd said it was delirium and morphine; he'd been in so much pain. But his wife, my aunt Nina, had heard him speak of it before and knew what he was saying. It was something that had happened when they were young, a secret Evan had kept from his sisters, something about my mother . . .

23

Discovery

I was in the minority, believing something had happened to her all those years ago, that all her savage pantomimes were coded to memories of real events. That first summer back in Arcadia, with my mother gone and Jenny just a year old, Elaine came to visit. We celebrated my birthday together. We talked, and she asked me then if I had ever heard the story her father told them just before he died.

Evan or his wife or *someone* had recounted it for his daughters, who were now grown women with husbands and children of their own.

They were remembering the last time they'd seen my mother, but they could have been talking about any number of occasions etched indelibly in our memories, when she would seem to transform herself before our very eyes. The way her episodes came on: a sudden, inexplicable change of mood. Unless you had been watching and listening to *everything* being said and every response, you could never be prepared. Then a tension in the room would have become so palpable you could cut it with a knife, like tripping the wire of some kind of trap. You could feel everyone suddenly freeze, caught off balance and casting about for their bearings.

Anyone who knew her well would know by then it was already too late; she would have made some remark, unable to control herself. Everyone would look up to see her capturing her "perpetrator" in a frozen gaze, and the inescapable explosion would follow: her inevitable accusations, hints of malevolence and betrayal, conspiracies and lies. Somehow, the contrast with her valiant attempts at propriety under normal, lucid circumstances created the greater part of the damage, by virtue of shock. When I was young it seemed to me as if people left her at these times, holding themselves in tatters, slashed here and there where she had broken away to cut wildly at all their delicate facades before they could even begin to realize what was happening and find cover. I remember still the hated sound of my father's voice while he tried to calm her. In my eyes, it made him an accomplice with the others, whom I had learned from earliest memory were not entirely free of guilt, though it pained me to see them wounded in this way. I wanted her not to care, to have protected herself from them. This was the lesson I had to learn for her, by myself, when I became a woman.

I had been standing by the window in my kitchen the first time I heard it, the story Elaine meant to tell. It was night, and Jenny was sleeping in her crib in her nursery, only a few months old. The phone rang, and I put it on my shoulder while I continued to clean up the dishes from our dinner. It was Ian; he had spoken to Elaine. They kept in touch across the long distance when she left California to go back to see her father. Ian was calling to ask me if our mother had ever said anything about a priest, when she and Evan were young together, in high school. Evan found out something about their priest and Marni, and there had been other girls, and he had been beside himself. He'd gone to confront the man, but then a strange episode happened, a meeting between the two of them alone—Evan and this man—and something about cigarettes. The priest had offered him a cigarette in his office, and Evan had been afraid . . . ?

I think I stopped moving at some point to listen. I remember I looked up then and noticed that the house next door was dark, no light in the windows across the way, where I was used to seeing movement at night. I felt that freezing inside, listening to my brother's voice, not of cold, but of stillness, of being utterly still and quiet, every cell seeming to hold itself motionless, listening.

"No, I never knew . . . she never said anything to me. I would *remember*."

I wanted to know why I was hearing it now, why they'd waited so long, why her whole life had gone by with us suffering, wondering what was wrong, and no one saying a word.

Years later, I repeat the story for Ian—Elaine's version as it was told to me that summer a year or two after my mother died, when I was alone with Jenny in LA. I asked him to try to remember what Elaine had told him before she talked with me. I try not to give details.

He says, "No, it wasn't like that . . . he didn't 'tell them' the story—it *came out*." He was psychotic from the morphine, he was dying. Elke or Dara, her sisters, had come to visit, he mistook them for Mom, he was hallucinating . . . it was a tirade, he was angry about something . . . and the whole story came out. Nina knew what he was saying; he had told her years before. He was angry with Mom and how they'd been intimidated by the clerics. The Sisters at the school had brought him in to find out exactly how much he knew. They'd reprimanded him for the cigarettes, they'd wanted to silence him; he felt humiliated. And it wasn't an "inappropriate advance"; it was sexual intercourse with young girls.

I try to imagine this for my mother at that age, but I can't. I just *cannot*.

24

Evan's Dream

He heard ringing—the sound of the train going by between his own farm and the neighboring farm, the fields where the horses . . . but there weren't any horses there now. The smoke from the smelter had killed the horses . . . the smelter and the sullen salt pond . . . someone had drowned there once—a boy . . .

He missed the fields, missed being outside, and soon winter would come. It was so quiet indoors in the afternoon. Even with Nina near, so quiet around him. But every time he looked out at the fields through the window by the bed he saw only that neighboring farm, the long red house and barns; and then he thought about her, alone inside that house with the kids at school during the day, those many years ago . . . what had happened to that baby, her baby? The story she had told them—the crow flying through the open window, and she so startled she'd dropped the baby, dropping the baby in the bath—that was what happened. But the baby had drowned.

These women . . . what had happened to them? They weren't like Nina . . . holding on to their secrets for so long it made the knowledge they hid grow like a cancer, harder and deeper, like cancers inside them. Now it was in him . . . but he'd tried *not* to . . . he'd tried not to hold all their secrets . . .

This place holding him now . . . they'd been here so long, so many years, the hill behind the house baking in the sun. And it seemed like only a short time ago that they had come there for the first time, and time had rushed past while they were young. Even now he could feel it, the hours passing, could smell the grasses and the damp of the thaw . . . the solid mass of earth and rock whose shelter the house had been built against. They found the arrowheads, still in the burial mounds, the sacred places in the hills above them. It had always been safe here, except . . . sometimes he'd have to leave, get away quickly, without a word to Nina or the girls, as far away as he could, anywhere. And then wandering, for days and weeks at a time, just to be safe . . . from what? He never quite knew . . . but he always came back, he wanted to come back, at least to be with them . . .

He had to come back; where else was there to go?

He felt the house shudder now. Outside the sky was a grayish blue. A storm had been sweeping through for days it seemed, the wind hitting the sides of the house and rushing through the trees and fields. He couldn't keep track of how long he'd been hearing it. But Nina knew, and she would tell him. Outside was a bank of thick white clouds now, cut into the sky like the edge of a cliff, the sun setting fire to its edges.

He heard music sometimes, the same song over and over. Underneath the layer of a slide guitar, so beautiful and mournful, the sound of running water in a rocky pool. How could that be? The stream . . . but he did . . . he did hear it.

A silver whirlpool was shining somewhere inside him, whirling and glinting at him from somewhere . . . and suddenly he saw the long silken fish lying on the sand alive, its body a paroxysm of hard white light.

The pain in his own body, making him remember the strangest things . . .

He didn't like to think of the trout now. He'd never go there again to fish the stream or anywhere ever again . . . never even leave this bed . . . so strange to think of that . . . he hadn't been able to make it let go of him, this thing that was slowly consuming him from within . . .

Now he'd never leave again . . . this time never come back . . . That whirlpool, covering something, something at the bottom . . . he couldn't see. . . . Now it seemed as though everything had been lying in wait for him all along, no choices in the hardest times, just stumbling into things that weren't right, that couldn't be made right, no way to turn back as if not knowing—all his life. He couldn't *take it* anymore, the waiting for something to happen, something real to blow up in his face. He couldn't anymore . . . the shellshock. They brought him back, they sent him to California . . . to Marni . . . and Don, for rest, and he did rest there.

But he could tell something about Marni . . . she was just biding time; she was waiting to get from one day to the next. Now he could see it better than he had then; it had started even before . . . when they were young . . . he had stumbled in again . . . something Naomi had said, in her typical wry way, looking at him with her head tilted to one side like a crow, and then everything hitting him at once.

They were in high school then. Marni had been in agony, of fear that their parents would find out, as though it were her fault that it had happened . . . a perfect victim. Evan didn't want to keep that secret . . . but the Sisters tried to make him afraid. He felt angry all of a sudden . . . they'd brought him in to find out what he knew, sounding him out, their perfect white faces and black clothes, the habits and vestments.

"Through the power vested in me by the Holy Spirit . . ."

Black cloth everywhere, for keeping secrets, for hiding things, for covering over everything—the innocent children and their secrets as well.

But they couldn't make him *not* know, couldn't undo that. Beneath all the blackness, he knew the secret, and so did others.

Some of the girls knew about Marni and the others, but no one spoke. They were all captives. No one said a word, as though they were held in . . . what was that word . . . ? *Thrall* . . . except Naomi. Naomi had spoken, but only to him. He was *so* angry, trying to make sense of what she was saying, the knowledge exploding inside him.

They made him pay for knowing, they made him squirm and feel afraid. The cigarettes . . . something about cigarettes . . . did he smoke? But they knew he smoked . . . he was so young then, but they were adults; he was afraid.

Hell, yeah, he smoked! He knew that was "wrong" . . . what did it have to do with this priest? And what he'd done to the girls, to *Marni* . . . it was wrong to accept the cigarettes . . . why were they asking him about smoking? . . . And who would believe him? . . . What were they prepared to do to him if he spoke?

"Putting the fear of God" in him . . . had there been a God then?

What was that word . . . as though they were held in . . . like "pall" . . . "appall". . . "pall bearers" . . .

Ah . . . it was 'thrall' . . .

He heard a whisper, "You mustn't drop the casket or the body will fall."

He felt tired now. It was hard to even remember hating them . . . he felt too tired to think about them anymore . . . but this might be the last time, the only chance he had left to remember . . . *something they had hidden* . . .

That sound . . . something was moving all around him, as though the room were moving, the bed very still at the center of something spinning everywhere . . . wind . . . or water? All his strength had gone, drained into a little pool of water he could hear bubbling now on the floor at the foot of his bed . . . the stream had come to him . . .

It was for her he kept quiet finally. It was the only right thing he could find; he thought she'd die of shame . . . she was such an innocent . . . he'd hated that, it was maddening, her trying to be . . . That was the trouble from the beginning—she believed all their crap . . .

Maybe he'd told her: "This is the body of Christ . . . ?"

She would never be able to bear it . . . how did they know that? She was never very good at truth.

"Truth is beauty, beauty is truth."

That's what they were taught. But she was only good at beauty, desperately unwilling to see anything else, and so much damage left behind. Will Darien be that way now too, holding on to innocence so blindly?

The priest had been sent away (on the QT) to serve in another parish, east somewhere . . . all very hush-hush . . . everyone knows how to do that.

The wind against the house made him feel as though the bed were rocking . . . the way they'd used to rock the girls when they were little . . .

"Hush-a-bye . . . don't you cry, go to sleepy little baby . . . when you wake . . . you shall find . . . all the pretty little horsies . . ."

She was waiting for him to come and be with her, to bring back all the hidden things, every secret . . . she'd made him promise . . . what good had it done? She'd gone before him, left him behind . . .

"But I won't . . . I won't come with you . . . I won't let you take me . . ."

She, holding out her hand again . . .

"Why did you . . . why couldn't you stop him?"

They don't like it . . . don't like what I'm saying . . . they don't want me to, someone doesn't want me to say . . .

"Please just let me, before it's too late . . . so much time gone by it won't matter anymore . . . please just . . ."

Everything suddenly moving so swiftly, sweeping him along like the surge of a current, he felt weightless with its whirling around him and wanting to be left behind. He tried to call out, but he couldn't make any sound. He tried to remember the sky, the daylight, the stars he knew were hidden somewhere behind that cover, a picture now, just in his mind . . .

He wasn't ready . . . the escort of the wind, so remorseless . . .

"It's the morphine."

"He said her name . . . he thinks she's Marni."

"She's not here, Evan . . . she's gone . . . it's Stacey here."

"Rest now."

25

The Forge

East Helena, Montana 1990

There would have been no way for Evan to know what to expect. And in place of that darkness, of his future waiting behind a curtain of time—in place of the dark blankness of not knowing what lay before him there was only a deeper darkness of panic, of terror even if he tried to imagine what it would be like, having already learned from listening to the stories of others, in other times, that it would be something beyond anything he could imagine.

He tried at first to compare, tried to think of the worst things he had seen in the war, but there was no point in that—those had been his undoing. At some point memory failed. He imagined a kind of pain he thought would grow and grow until it became all of him, until the small, silent voice that he had always clung to as himself, whatever could defy that consuming force would be extinguished, and all his awareness of it would be over, finally, and only traces left of whatever he had been, for others to remember.

He did not even worry about death itself just yet. He did not want to call out, and he did not want them to watch him suffer as he had had to watch others suffer, feeling helpless.

How did it go? . . . "And they shall be as eagles . . ."

"They . . . shall renew their strength; they shall mount up with wings as eagles; they shall run and not be weary; and they shall walk, and not faint."

But it would be different finally, though at first as he had feared, however mistaken in his fear. Still, it had been true that it was nothing he could ever imagine for himself. And he realized then that he could never have allowed himself to imagine much of the best or the worst of his life.

He did not believe he would know when it began, and when finally it was there in earnest, he watched himself silently, reading the messages of each sensation and measuring the pain against an image of himself he had adopted in his mind—a piece of coal glowing red in a furnace, the pain becoming brighter and brighter, the color moving and flickering, taking on the simple shape of the confines of his body, contained as it was from the rest of the room that he had once known existed, the burning blackness searching everywhere inside him until he would know what it was to be only a fuel for that flame—his body, his mind all reduced to that and memory.

But in the end, it was not like that, not like that rough and simple piece of coal he had imagined as himself—that would burn until the burning thing that fed on him burned finally away. Something changed, and so, in his imagination, the picture of himself changed too. And instead of the fine silver powder of ashes—all his past reduced to that, like bits of snow and cloud that crumbled and broke against each other, like the powdery wings of moths; instead of that, something else happened.

And in the burning that he had watched as well as he could without growing faint, in that burning that had once been a kind of torment, he began instead to hear a soft whispering, like the hiss of the pieces of iron in the cool water, a soft sighing, the sigh of each cell of his body singing its memory in the coolness left to it when the colors were gone, when there was just enough of himself still left to know that he had been released.

Sympathy

My sister ships can no longer receive my signals, and the vessels that move nearer by have shut themselves down for this dark night. My distress calls fly further afield, into a perfect darkness, and the flares above my bow are mistaken for signs of celebration. I have heard that there are safer waters, but I've only the place of my maiden voyage in memory now, where, unsuspecting, someplace below the surface, I tear myself against a shadow, waiting silent and unmoving in the ice fields.

Some time elapsed before I realized I was sinking, heading for the bottom, and no one was going there with me. Those closest to me, resting their hopes on my strength, acquire expressions of panic, inevitably throwing themselves from my decks, while others, trying to maintain their equilibrium in the face of death, adopt a pretense and play on gallantly while I take on water.

I am spoken of as a "survivor," though the word assumes another meaning now and comes to represent, in my heart, not a picture of my wholeness, of resting undaunted on the cradle of the waves, but rather enduring in darkness, beneath all that moves above in the world of man, silently at the bottom of the sea, in the company of mute and primitive creatures whose delicate bodies are able to withstand the pressure of this abyss.

Halloween 1997

In my dream, we are flying above an ancient forest of oak. A euphoria that borders on madness has lent us wings. Tracks of silent streams are gleaming below, but there is no moon. The animals see us. They stop their movements to watch, just as in life, except that they judge us safe and turn back to continue their nighttime vigils. We make a dance of our flight, in dives and ascents through branches heavy with witch's broom. The air is electrified with our gladness, a silent laughter that remains eternally unheard.

Among the trees the stone walls of an old house guard a light within, but the laughter from inside spills out on the air to beckon us. All around, the anticipation of former evenings envelops us. Only tonight, somehow, I know the revelry will end differently.

I have the longing for darkness that has been spoken of elsewhere, a yearning to find the place I dream about in that ancient grove: the stone house standing there. Not just to see them, but to live again whatever it was that happened I cannot remember.

I take a bicycle to the path by the water; the dragonflies and velvet-black bees become an escort. We fly along in separate streams, above the rocky ledge that meets a gray and windy sea, as though a channel enveloped us, a slipstream, and left a window on the salt and sunlight. And the wind is all around me. And my body becomes the body of the black cormorant who stares with such concentrated stillness out over the water. And I watch the snowy egrets if the water is low, and sometimes by accident the night heron, who mislays his disguise. And I think of the shining, wide-eyed dances of the stone-colored rays just below the waves. And I want to be with them.

When you died, I could not think how to find you. Longing for you, I called out silently in the fear and pain of my first time in labor, and the many years of separateness melted away. Trying to bring my own child, I was yours again, your little girl. Wanting only to feel you beside me as in lost and cherished times when you comforted me merely by being near.

There was only darkness and a black wall of stars. I was willing to find you anywhere but discovered only the silent emptiness. I don't want that for Jenny.

I want her to know where to look.

So, this: look by the water where the birds are, where the waves beckon, just below in the darkness where the rays are dancing, on the sun-burning ledge where the hawk is riding motionless above, with the women who come down to the river on bare feet in the dry Coptic sun. I have longed for the darkness of another place and time. But always to be with her and her father, as we were at the very beginning. That memory does not die.

Coal Miner's Daughter

At some point in my twenties, shortly after graduation, I stumbled upon a photograph in a book of documentary work by Marion Post Wolcott, a photographer for the Farm Securities Administration under FDR.

It's a picture taken from the back, of a little girl in the middle distance, about nine years of age, wearing a tattered calico dress and carrying a pail down a narrow dirt track that runs between clapboard houses on the right and the train tracks on the left. The tracks are not visible because, as though mirroring in sympathy the burdened progress of the little girl, they are carrying a line of cars filled to overflowing with the coal from the same mines where the child's father labors. The little girl advances toward what one assumes is "home" or her men folk in the camp somewhere in the distance. Where the coal is going, we only imagine is far away.

When I look at that photo, I remember the stories my mother's sisters told, of her bringing a pail just like this to their father, with his lunch or his water, through the town at midday, or coming to get him from the bar at twilight. The little girl's hair is cut just below her ears; she's thin and strains against the weight of the pail that is shouldered all to one side. One feels sure she is oblivious to the fact that she is becoming an important part of the photograph if she noticed the photographer at all. She's about the same age as my mother would have been in that year, 1938, and she looks to be in about the same kind of place.

When I look at that photograph, it's as though natural laws have reversed themselves and I have a chance, as an adult, to look back into a moment in time that occurred before I was born. And all I see is my mother, only her little child self and the life into which she was born. As always, I want to help her. I want to comfort her. Only I know what her future holds.

W hat if one were to realize all at once that the world of the past, of memory and dreams, was more real, somehow more important to one's survival than the events of one's daily life?

She dreams of bridges, of driving across the ones she knows. She's never been afraid before, but now in the dreams strange, magical happenings unfold.

One night at the Golden Gate, the span carries her underwater where she discovers long-lost friends, all sitting at high tea at a beautiful table at the bottom of the bay; only it was long ago, and everyone, even she, is in Victorian dress.

In another dream the bridge does not yet exist. Where the beautiful city would grow are only sandstone cliffs and desert, and she is just spirit, flying above the water.

But in most of the dreams she is driving. Her eyelids become heavy, she can't see the road, she knows she's going to faint. She struggles to keep control of the car but can feel herself falling, slipping toward the floor, the vehicle breaking over the railing, carrying her with it under the water.

The dreams recur so often that she begins to relive them while awake. She becomes afraid of heights, of driving over the railing into the waves. Then just as suddenly, the dreams stop. Years go by, until the day she hears that he's jumped, when she remembers them again.

Acknowledgments

I would like to thank the following friends, associates, employers, and others who have extended their support and encouragement over the years, and whose presence in my life helped me to value my artistic efforts, especially this memoir—since I first began the project.

I am indebted to the faculty and staff of the following institutions: [The former] Mills College, in particular to Ron Nagle, Catherine Wagner, and John Chambers; and the faculty of their graduate teaching program, esp. Linda Kroll, Vicki Labosky, Ruth Cosey; the San Francisco Art Institute, esp. to Linda Connor; to Dominican University of San Rafael, especially Sister Joanne Cullimore and Foad Satterfield—the example of their own work, their dedication to (and encouragement of) their students, were invaluable to me; the Dominican Sisters and faculty of the Santa Catalina School in Monterey, for their generous offer of scholarship funds for my daughter and for the caliber of their teaching and their dedication to a special environment for educating young women; the faculty, staff, and administration of Alverno High School, for their kindness and dedication: their school provided needed stability, inspiration, and enrichment to me in the year before I first left home; the faculty and staff of Santa Cruz High School, especially Mr. Robert Davenport, who introduced his students to the beautiful writing of the Southern Regional American authors.

To my employers in my work with families privately, for their esteem and support in entrusting to me the care of their children, whose personalities and lives so deeply enriched my own and continue to inspire and amaze me.

To Scott Brandt, PhD and Bob Goodnough, PhD, with whom I worked over the years to integrate the memories of my early life while navigating marriage, motherhood, and practicing the vocation I have loved most.

To dear and loyal friends, including Ana Gordon, Deborah Johnson, Francis Whitnall, Linda Moore, Norma Gomez, Sofia Salamanca, Terry Grove, and Yvonne Obenchain, and to Louise Music, for her collegiality and friendship during our college years.

A special note of thanks to the friend who has known me the longest, Dr. LeeAnn Bartolini, for her constancy and wisdom, which made her the only person (for decades) with whom I felt safe to share my writing. Her encouragement and belief in me have been a guiding light, without which this book may not have come into being.

To my late aunt Myrtle (nee Bratvold) Marcinkowski, who courageously opened her home to me when first I left the one where I had grown up. And to my older sister and brother who, while still so young themselves, both recognized my vulnerability as the youngest child and undertook to "parent" me as best they could while I was still living at home and later, after leaving home. You are both a large reason for this dream being realized.

And finally, to my daughter, Natalie, the greatest gift in my life, and to her father.

About the Author

Kristen Alexandra Davis grew up in a suburb in the San Gabriel Valley of Southern California. She holds a master's degree in early childhood education and has worked in both private/ home settings as a nanny and also in elementary school settings as a teacher and teaching assistant. Prior to that, while raising her daughter as a single mother, she worked in the historic fine art photography galleries in Carmel, California, representing the work of some of the main artists in the field—Ansel Adams, Edward and Brett Weston, Imogen Cunningham, and other more contemporary artists. She now lives in Northern California, where she enjoys exploring beautiful hiking trails and spending time near the water.

SELECTED TITLES FROM SHE WRITES PRESS

She Writes Press is an independent publishing
company founded to serve women writers everywhere.
Visit us at www.shewritespress.com.

Seeing Eye Girl: A Memoir of Madness, Resilience, and Hope by Beverly J. Armento. $16.95, 978-1-64742-391-9. Written for the invisible walking wounded among us who hide their pain behind smile—and for the educators and mentors who sometimes doubt the power of their influence—*Seeing Eye Girl* is an inspiring story of one girl's search for hope in an abusive, dysfunctional home, and of the teachers who empowered her.

Singing with the Sirens: Overcoming the Long-Term Effects of Childhood Sexual Exploitation by Ellyn Bell and Stacey Bell. $16.95, 978-1-63152-936-8. With metaphors of sea creatures and the force of the ocean as a backdrop, this work addresses the problems of sexual abuse and exploitation of young girls, taking the reader on a poetic journey toward finding healing from within.

Now I Can See the Moon: A Story of a Social Panic, False Memories, and a Life Cut Short by Alice Tallmadge. $16.95, 978-1-63152-330-4. A first-person account from inside the bizarre and life-shattering social panic over child sex abuse that swept through the US in the 1980s—and affected Alice Tallmadge's family in a personal, devastating way.

Raising Myself: A Memoir of Neglect, Shame, and Growing Up Too Soon by Beverly Engel. $16.95, 978-1-63152-367-0. A powerfully inspiring and unflinchingly honest story of how best-selling author and abuse recovery expert Beverly Engel made her way in the world—in spite of her mother's neglect and constant criticism, undergoing sexual abuse at nine, and being raped at twelve.

Secrets in Big Sky Country: A Memoir by Mandy Smith. $16.95, 978-1-63152-814-9. A bold and unvarnished memoir about the shattering consequences of familial sexual abuse—and the strength it takes to overcome them.

The Sergeant's Daughter: A Memoir by Teressa Shelton. $16.95, 978-1-63152-721-0. Every night of her childhood life, Teressa's sergeant father brings his military life home, meeting each of his daughters' infractions with extreme punishment for them all. At first cowed by her father's abuse and desperate to believe that maybe, one day, things will change, Teressa ultimately grows into a young woman who understands that if she wants a better life, she'll have to build it for herself—so she does.